DIGITAL DETOX MADE EASY

A COMPREHENSIVE PRACTICAL GUIDE FOR EVERYONE

DR. NITNEM SINGH SODHI

Made with ♥ on the Notion Press Platform
www.notionpress.com

Dedicated to my loving father.

Contents

Preface

Welcome to "Digital Detox Made Easy: A Comprehensive Practical Guide for Everyone," a book that is designed to help you take control of your relationship with technology and lead a more fulfilling and productive life. As we become more and more reliant on technology, it's easy to lose sight of the impact it has on our mental well-being and productivity. In this book, I have included all the essential information you need to understand the effects of technology on our mental health and how to set healthy boundaries to ensure that technology enhances our lives rather than controls them. I have also provided a step-by-step guide to crafting your own personalized digital detox plan, along with a one-week and a two-week detox plan to help you get started.

Throughout the book, I have drawn on my experience to provide a comprehensive and practical guide to digital detox that is grounded in psychology and neuroscience. I believe that by taking a holistic approach to our relationship with technology, we can build a healthier, more fulfilling life. I hope that this book will inspire you to take the necessary steps to reclaim your life from the overwhelming influence of technology and lead a more balanced and fulfilling life. Thank you for joining me on this journey.

Dr. Nitnem Singh Sodhi

About The Author

Dr. Nitnem Singh Sodhi is a distinguished psychologist, neuroscientist, and renowned author. He has successfully treated numerous patients struggling with a variety of mental health issues and is recognized by the India Book of Records and Asia Book of Records as the world's youngest neuro-psychologist.

In his groundbreaking book, "Develop Immunity for Mental Health: A Comprehensive Practical Guide for Everyone," Dr. Sodhi offers readers coping mechanisms to manage and heal all types of psychological problems and detailed guidance on common mental health issues. With this latest book, "Digital Detox Made Easy: A Comprehensive Practical Guide for Everyone," Dr. Sodhi provides a comprehensive and practical guide to help individuals break free from their digital addiction and reclaim their lives. The book includes core concepts and practical aspects of digital detox and a one-week and a two-week digital detox plan, crafted based on the principles taught in the book. Readers can also learn to craft their own digital detox plan, best suited to their needs and goals.

Dr. Sodhi's research work, "The Unimind Metamodel" and "Thc Unibrain Theory," has revolutionized the field of psychology and neuroscience by providing the world's first unified model/framework of mind and brain. He has also developed innovative systems of therapy for the treatment of mental health disorders and has been a speaker at TEDx. Highly respected in the field of mental health, Dr. Sodhi's clinical practice has helped thousands of patients achieve complete healing within just a few psychotherapy sessions, without any medications. His latest book, "Digital Detox

Made Easy," is a must-read for anyone seeking to break free from their digital addiction and achieve a balanced and fulfilling life.

CHAPTER ONE

Introduction to Digital Detox

In this digital era, we are constantly bombarded with information, notifications, and distractions from our electronic devices. Social media, emails, text messages, and other online activities significantly consume our time and attention, leaving lesser room for real-life experiences and meaningful connections. This is where digital detox comes in. Digital detox is a term used to describe the process of intentionally disconnecting from technology in order to improve one's mental and physical health. It involves taking a break from our devices, such as smartphones, computers, and tablets, in order to reduce the negative effects of excessive technology use on our wellbeing. The concept of digital detox has gained popularity in recent years due to the growing awareness of the negative impact that technology can have on our lives. From decreased attention spans and disrupted sleep patterns to increased stress and anxiety, the negative effects of excessive technology use are well-documented.

Digital detox can take many forms, depending on the individual's needs and goals. It can be as simple as taking a break from social media for a few days, or as comprehensive as a complete disconnection from technology for an extended period of time. The purpose of digital detox is to give our brains a break from the constant stimulation and distraction that technology provides. It provides an opportunity to disconnect from the constant barrage of notifications, emails, and social media updates and focus on other aspects of our lives, such as spending time with loved ones, pursuing hobbies, or simply enjoying nature. Some of the benefits of digital detox include improved sleep, reduced stress and anxiety, increased productivity, and improved overall mental and physical health. It can also lead to increased creativity, as it allows our brains to rest and recharge.

It is important to note that digital detox is not about demonizing technology or completely disconnecting from it altogether. Rather, it is about finding a healthy balance between our technology use and other aspects of our lives. It is about being intentional with our technology use, setting boundaries, and taking breaks when necessary. It is is simple a process of intentionally disconnecting from technology in order to improve our overall wellbeing. It involves taking a break from our devices and focusing on other aspects of our lives. It is important to find a healthy balance between our technology use and other areas of our lives in order to maintain a healthy relationship with technology

Digital detox can take many different forms, from simply turning off your phone for a few hours to taking a full week away from all electronic devices. The key is to disconnect from technology in a deliberate and intentional way. This can be challenging, as our devices have become so integral to our daily routines and habits. The concept of digital detox is not new. In fact, it has been around for several years, with people recognizing the negative effects of digital overload on their mental and physical health. Digital overload refers to the state of being overwhelmed by the constant stimulation and information overload from electronic devices. It can lead to stress, anxiety, and a decreased ability to focus and concentrate.

There are several reasons why digital detox is important, ranging from mental health to physical health to productivity. Let's explore these in more detail.

- Improved Mental Health

The constant use of technology can take a toll on our mental health, leading to increased stress, anxiety, and depression. Studies have shown that excessive screen time can have a negative impact on our mental well-being, particularly in children and adolescents (Twenge, 2019). By taking a break from technology through a digital detox, we can reduce our exposure to these negative effects and improve our overall mood. We can reconnect with the present moment and focus on the people and experiences around us, rather than being consumed by our screens.

- Better Sleep

Exposure to the blue light emitted by electronic devices can interfere with our body's natural sleep cycle. This can lead to difficulty falling asleep, staying asleep, and feeling rested in the morning. Research has shown that even a single exposure to blue light at night can suppress the production of melatonin, a hormone that regulates sleep (Cajochen et al., 2011). By reducing our exposure to electronic devices through a digital detox, we can improve our sleep quality and feel more rested in the morning. This can have a positive impact on our overall health and well-being.

- Increased Productivity

It may seem counterintuitive, but taking a break from technology can actually increase our productivity. When we are constantly distracted by notifications and messages, it can be difficult to focus on the task at hand. This can lead to decreased productivity and increased stress. By disconnecting from technology through a digital detox, we can create a more focused and productive work environment. We can prioritize our tasks and devote our full attention to them, without the distractions of our devices.

- Improved Physical Health

The overuse of technology can also have negative effects on our physical health. Sitting for extended periods of time in front of screens can lead to a sedentary lifestyle and increased risk of obesity, diabetes, and heart disease (Katzmarzyk et al., 2009). By taking a break from technology through a digital detox, we can encourage more physical activity and reduce our risk of these health problems. We can engage in outdoor activities, exercise, and other forms of movement that promote physical health.

- Improved Relationships

Our constant use of technology can also have a negative impact on our relationships. We may feel disconnected from the people around us, even when we are physically present with them. We may prioritize our screens over face-to-face interactions, leading to a lack of intimacy and connection. By taking a break from technology through a digital detox, we can improve our relationships with others. We can focus on meaningful conversations and interactions, without the distractions of our devices. This can lead to deeper connections and a greater sense of community.

Here is a long list of benefits of digital detox to help you understand more about Digital Detox :

1. Reduced stress and anxiety - Studies have shown that excessive screen time can lead to increased stress and anxiety levels. Taking a break from technology can help reduce these negative emotions.
2. Improved mental health and mood - Research has shown that excessive screen time is linked to poor mental health outcomes such as depression, anxiety, and addiction. A digital detox can help improve mood and overall mental health.
3. Increased productivity and creativity - Too much screen time can lead to decreased productivity and creativity. A digital detox can help to improve these skills.
4. Better sleep quality and quantity - Exposure to blue light from electronic devices can interfere with our sleep-wake cycle, leading to poor sleep quality and quantity. A digital detox can help to improve sleep.

5. Enhanced physical health and fitness - Too much screen time can lead to physical inactivity, which is linked to a range of health problems. A digital detox can encourage physical activity and improve physical health.
6. Improved relationships with others - Excessive screen time can lead to feelings of disconnection from others. A digital detox can help improve relationships with friends and family.
7. Increased mindfulness and present moment awareness - Constant distraction from digital devices can make it difficult to be present in the moment. A digital detox can improve mindfulness and present moment awareness.
8. Decreased dependence on technology - Overreliance on digital technology can be harmful. A digital detox can help reduce dependence on technology.
9. Reduced risk of addiction to technology - Digital addiction is a real problem that can lead to a range of negative outcomes. A digital detox can help reduce the risk of addiction.
10. Increased face-to-face interactions and social connections - Too much screen time can lead to decreased social connections. A digital detox can encourage face-to-face interactions and improve social connections.
11. More time for self-reflection and personal growth - Digital overload can leave little time for self-reflection and personal growth. A digital detox can create space for these important activities.
12. Increased sense of balance and fulfillment in life - A digital detox can help create a more balanced and fulfilling life.

13. Enhanced cognitive function and focus - Too much screen time can lead to decreased cognitive function and focus. A digital detox can help improve these skills.
14. Increased ability to manage time and priorities - Overreliance on digital technology can make it difficult to manage time and priorities. A digital detox can improve these skills.
15. Improved memory and information retention - Research has shown that excessive screen time can lead to decreased memory and information retention. A digital detox can help improve these skills.
16. Greater clarity and purpose in life - Digital overload can make it difficult to find clarity and purpose in life. A digital detox can help create space for these important goals.
17. Reduced eye strain and headaches - Excessive screen time can lead to eye strain and headaches. A digital detox can reduce the risk of these problems.
18. Improved posture and reduced risk of musculoskeletal problems - Excessive screen time can lead to poor posture and musculoskeletal problems. A digital detox can reduce the risk of these problems.
19. Greater appreciation for nature and the outdoors - Too much screen time can make it difficult to appreciate the natural world. A digital detox can encourage appreciation for nature and the outdoors.
20. Increased creativity and innovation - Excessive screen time can lead to decreased creativity and innovation. A digital detox can help improve these skills.
21. More time for hobbies and interests - Digital overload can leave little time for hobbies and interests. A digital detox can create space for these important activities.

22. Improved overall well-being and quality of life - A digital detox can improve overall well-being and quality of life.
23. Increased sense of control and agency over one's life - Digital overload can make it feel like technology is controlling our lives. A digital detox can help regain a sense of control and agency.
24. Greater self-awareness and introspection - Digital overload can make it difficult to be introspective and self-aware. A digital detox can create space for self-reflection and greater self-awareness.

What digital detox is not :

In recent years, there has been a growing trend towards digital detoxing, which involves taking a break from digital technology to improve mental and physical health. While this can be an effective way to reduce stress and improve well-being, there are some misconceptions about what digital detoxing entails. In this article, we will explore what digital detoxing is not, and examine some of the myths surrounding this practice.

Myth 1: Digital detoxing means cutting off all digital technology

One of the most common misconceptions about digital detoxing is that it involves completely cutting off all digital technology. However, this is not necessarily the case. While some people may choose to go completely offline for a period of time, digital detoxing can also involve reducing or limiting the use of certain digital technologies, such as social media, email, or smartphones. The goal is not to eliminate all technology but to use it more mindfully and intentionally.

Myth 2: Digital detoxing is a one-time event

Another misconception about digital detoxing is that it is a one-time event. However, true digital detoxing involves making lasting changes to your relationship with digital technology. This may involve adopting new habits or routines that prioritize self-care and balance, such as taking regular breaks from screens, setting boundaries around technology use, or engaging in offline activities that bring you joy and fulfillment.

Myth 3: Digital detoxing is only for people with addiction

Another common myth about digital detoxing is that it is only for people with a digital addiction. While excessive use of digital technology can certainly be problematic for some individuals, digital detoxing is not solely for those with addiction. Anyone can benefit from taking a break from technology to reduce stress, improve mental health, and reconnect with the world around them.

Myth 4: Digital detoxing means giving up all the benefits of technology

Many people are hesitant to try digital detoxing because they fear they will miss out on the benefits of technology, such as staying connected with friends and family or accessing important information. However, digital detoxing does not have to mean giving up all the benefits of technology. It simply means using technology in a more mindful and intentional way, so that it enhances rather than detracts from our lives.

Myth 5: Digital detoxing is easy

Finally, there is a misconception that digital detoxing is easy. However, like any lifestyle change, it can be challenging to break old habits and adopt new ones. It can be especially difficult in a world where digital technology is so pervasive and often essential for work, school, and social life. However, with persistence and support, it is possible to make lasting changes to your relationship with digital technology and reap the benefits of digital detoxing.

Thus, we can conclude that digital detoxing is a valuable practice for improving mental and physical health, but there are some misconceptions about what it entails. It is not about completely cutting off all digital technology or engaging in a one-time event, nor is it only for those with addiction. Rather, it involves making lasting changes to your relationship with technology that prioritize self-care and balance. By dispelling these myths and embracing the benefits of digital detoxing, we can lead healthier, happier, and more connected lives.

CHAPTER TWO

Impact of Technology on Our Lives

Digital technology has revolutionized the way we live, work, and communicate. From smartphones and social media to cloud computing and artificial intelligence, digital technology has had a profound impact on our daily lives. In this article, we will explore the various ways in which digital technology has transformed our lives and examine both the benefits and challenges it presents.

- Communication: One of the most significant impacts of digital technology has been on communication. With the rise of social media platforms like Facebook, Twitter, Instagram, and TikTok, people can now communicate with each other instantly, regardless of their physical location. This has made it easier for us to stay in touch with family and friends, share news, and connect with like-minded individuals around the world. However, the constant stream of information can also be overwhelming, leading to information overload and digital burnout.

- Work: Digital technology has also transformed the workplace. With the advent of remote work and video conferencing tools like Zoom and Skype, employees can now work from anywhere in the world. This has made it easier for companies to access a global talent pool and reduce costs associated with office space and commuting. However, remote work can also lead to feelings of isolation and disconnection from colleagues, and it can be challenging to maintain work-life balance when your office is just a few steps away from your living room.

- Education: Digital technology has had a significant impact on education. With the rise of online learning platforms like Coursera, Udemy, and edX, students can now access educational materials from anywhere in the world. This has made education more accessible and affordable, particularly for those who live in remote areas or cannot afford to attend traditional brick-and-mortar schools. However, online learning can also be challenging for some students who require in-person interaction with teachers and classmates to fully understand the material.

- Entertainment: Digital technology has transformed the way we consume entertainment. With the rise of streaming services like Netflix, Hulu, and Amazon Prime Video, we can now access a vast library of movies, TV shows, and documentaries from the comfort of our homes. This has made it easier for us to binge-watch our favorite shows, discover new content, and avoid traditional advertising. However, this convenience can also lead to sedentary lifestyles and social isolation, as we spend more time in front of screens and less time engaging with the outside world.

- Health: Digital technology has also had an impact on our physical and mental health. Wearable devices like Fitbit and Apple Watch can track our fitness levels, monitor our sleep patterns, and provide real-time feedback on our health. This has made it easier for us to stay active and make healthier choices. However, the constant use of digital devices can also lead to eye strain, neck pain, and other physical ailments. Additionally, social media and other digital platforms can contribute to feelings of anxiety, depression, and FOMO (fear of missing out), leading to negative impacts on our mental health.

- Privacy and Security: Digital technology has also raised concerns about privacy and security. With the amount of personal information we share online, there is a risk of identity theft, cyberbullying, and other forms of digital abuse. Additionally, the use of artificial intelligence and machine learning algorithms has raised concerns about bias and discrimination in decision-making processes. It is essential to remain vigilant about protecting our personal information and advocating for policies that protect our privacy and security in the digital age.

Hence, digital technology has had a profound impact on our lives, bringing both benefits and challenges. While it has made communication, work, education, entertainment, and health more accessible and convenient, it has also raised concerns about privacy, security, and mental and physical health. As we continue to embrace digital technology, it is crucial to remain aware of its impacts and work to address the challenges it presents while maximizing its benefits. This can be achieved through responsible use of digital technology, advocating for policies that protect privacy and security, and staying informed about emerging trends and risks. By doing so, we can harness the power of digital technology to enhance our lives and create a more connected, inclusive, and equitable society.

Social media platforms have rapidly risen in popularity over the past decade. In 2005, Facebook was launched, and it quickly gained traction as a way for college students to connect and share information. Over the next several years, Facebook expanded to include people of all ages and became one of the most widely used social media platforms in the world. Other platforms, such as Twitter and Instagram, also gained popularity, offering unique features that appealed to different audiences. The rise of social media has brought many benefits, such as the ability to connect with friends and family across the world, and the opportunity to share our thoughts, feelings, and experiences with a wide audience. Social media has also been a powerful tool for activism, allowing people to organize and mobilize around important issues.

However, social media has also been linked to a number of negative effects on mental health. One of the biggest concerns is the potential for addiction. Social media is designed to be engaging and addictive, with notifications and likes triggering the release of dopamine in the brain. This creates a feeling of reward, which can make it difficult to put down our devices and disconnect from social media. Research has shown that people who use social media frequently may be more likely to experience symptoms of depression, anxiety, and other mental health problems. Social media use has been linked to feelings of loneliness and social isolation, as well as a decreased sense of well-being. Studies have also found that people who spend more time on social media are more likely to experience negative emotions, such as envy, frustration, and anger. One reason social media may be linked to negative mental health outcomes is because it presents an idealized version of life. People tend to share only their most positive experiences and accomplishments on social media, which can make it difficult for others to keep up. This can lead to feelings of inadequacy and low self-esteem, as people compare themselves to others and feel that they don't measure up.

Social media has also been linked to cyberbullying, which can have serious negative effects on mental health. Cyberbullying can take many forms, from name-calling and teasing to more serious forms of harassment and threats. Victims of cyberbullying may experience depression, anxiety, and other mental health problems, and may be at increased risk for suicidal thoughts and behaviors.

We can understand that the social media can be a source of information overload, leading to feelings of overwhelm and stress. With so much information available at our fingertips, it can be difficult to know what to focus on and what to ignore. This can lead to a constant sense of distraction, making it difficult to relax and unwind. While social media has many advantages, it's important to acknowledge its potential negative effects on our mental health. Practicing balance and healthy habits in our social media use can help prevent negative impacts.

Screen time refers to the amount of time that we spend in front of screens, such as smartphones, tablets, computers, and televisions. While screens have become an integral part of our daily lives, research suggests that excessive screen time can have negative effects on both physical and mental health.

Physical Effects:

- Poor Sleep: Screen time can disrupt our natural sleep patterns by delaying the release of melatonin, a hormone that regulates sleep. This can make it difficult to fall asleep, stay asleep, and wake up feeling rested.
- Eye Strain: Staring at screens for extended periods of time can cause eye strain, dry eyes, and headaches.
- Posture: Poor posture when using screens can lead to neck and back pain, and may even cause long-term spinal problems.
- Obesity: Excessive screen time has been linked to an increased risk of obesity, as it often involves sedentary behavior and snacking while watching screens.

Mental Effects:

- Depression and Anxiety: Studies have found a link between excessive screen time and symptoms of depression and anxiety. This may be due to the social isolation that can come from spending too much time online, as well as the negative emotions that can arise from comparing oneself to others on social media.
- Addiction: Like social media, screens can be addictive, with the constant stimulation of new information and

activities triggering the release of dopamine in the brain. This can make it difficult to put down our devices and can lead to compulsive behavior.

- Impaired Brain Development: Excessive screen time in children has been linked to impaired brain development, particularly in areas of the brain responsible for language, literacy, and attention.
- Decreased Social Skills: Spending too much time online can lead to a lack of social interaction and may decrease social skills, particularly in children who are still developing these skills.

In addition to these specific effects, excessive screen time can also have a negative impact on overall well-being, as it can lead to feelings of stress, overwhelm, and a constant sense of being "plugged in."

It's important to note that not all screen time is created equal. Some screen time, such as educational apps and programs, can be beneficial, particularly for children. However, it's important to practice moderation and balance when it comes to screen time, and to be aware of the potential negative effects that excessive screen time can have on our physical and mental health.

Technology overuse can lead to sleep disruption through a variety of mechanisms. One of the primary ways that technology impacts sleep is by disrupting the body's circadian rhythm, which is the internal "clock" that regulates the sleep-wake cycle. Exposure to blue light from electronic devices such as smartphones and laptops can suppress the production of the sleep-inducing hormone melatonin, which can make it harder to fall asleep and stay asleep. The impact of technology on sleep is not limited to the blue light emitted by electronic devices. The content and activities people engage in on their devices can also contribute to sleep disruption. For example, social media platforms are designed to be engaging and stimulating, which can increase cognitive arousal and make it harder to unwind and fall asleep. The constant availability of technology can also lead to a sense of FOMO (fear of missing out) and make it difficult for individuals to disconnect from their devices and prioritize sleep. The relationship between technology and sleep disruption is bidirectional, meaning that poor sleep can also lead to increased technology use. When people are sleep-deprived, they may be more likely to rely on technology as a way to stay awake or manage their fatigue. However, this can create a cycle of technology use and sleep disruption, leading to a further decline in overall sleep quality.

The impact of technology on sleep disruption is particularly concerning for children and adolescents. Research has shown that screen time in the hours leading up to bedtime is associated with later bedtimes, shorter sleep duration, and decreased sleep quality in children and adolescents. This can have significant negative effects on physical and mental health, including increased risk of obesity, poor academic performance, and mental health problems such as depression and anxiety. Overall, the link between technology and sleep disruption is complex and multifaceted, and it is an area of ongoing research. However, it is clear that excessive technology use, particularly in the hours leading up to bedtime, can have a significant impact on sleep quality and overall health and well-being.

CHAPTER THREE

Identify When You Need a Digital Detox

As our lives become increasingly intertwined with technology, it can be difficult to know when we need to take a break from our devices. However, there are several signs that can indicate a need for a digital detox. Here are some symptoms to look out for:

1. Constantly checking your phone or other electronic devices, even when there are no notifications or alerts.
2. Feeling anxious or agitated when you are away from your devices.
3. Having trouble focusing or staying on task due to constant interruptions from technology.
4. Feeling like you are missing out on important updates or events because you are not checking your devices.
5. Experiencing physical symptoms such as headaches, eye strain, or neck pain from prolonged screen time.
6. Feeling drained or fatigued, even if you have not engaged in any physical activity.
7. Having trouble falling asleep or staying asleep due to the blue light emitted by electronic devices.

8. Feeling like you have lost control of your technology use, and that it is taking up too much of your time and energy.
9. Experiencing social isolation or feelings of loneliness due to spending too much time on social media or other digital platforms.
10. Feeling like you have lost touch with the natural world or your own creativity due to constant engagement with technology.
11. Feeling like you are constantly comparing yourself to others on social media, and experiencing negative emotions as a result.
12. Struggling to form deep, meaningful connections with others due to relying too heavily on digital communication.
13. Feeling like your attention span has decreased, and finding it difficult to focus on anything for an extended period of time.
14. Experiencing a decrease in productivity due to being constantly distracted by technology.
15. Finding that you are spending more and more money on technology and digital services, and feeling like you cannot live without them.
16. Experiencing feelings of boredom or restlessness when you are not engaging with technology.
17. Feeling like you are constantly "on call" for work or other obligations due to the constant access provided by technology.
18. Feeling like your personal privacy is constantly being violated, and struggling to protect your personal information from being collected and shared by technology companies.

19. Experiencing symptoms of depression or anxiety that are worsened by your use of technology.
20. Feeling like you have lost touch with your own sense of identity, and that your digital presence has become more important than your real-life relationships and experiences.

If you are experiencing any of these symptoms, it may be time to consider a digital detox. By taking a break from technology, you can give yourself the space and freedom to reconnect with your true self and the world around you.

Technology has become an integral part of our daily lives, but for some individuals, the use of technology can become problematic or even addictive. Addiction to technology can interfere with daily functioning and have negative effects on mental health, relationships, and overall well-being.

Here are some common signs of addiction to technology:

1. Compulsive use: Feeling like you cannot control your use of technology, and using it more often and for longer periods of time than you intended.
2. Tolerance: Needing to use technology more and more in order to get the same level of satisfaction or pleasure.
3. Withdrawal: Feeling irritable, anxious, or restless when you are unable to use technology, such as when your phone battery dies or you do not have access to Wi-Fi.

4. Loss of interest: Losing interest in other activities that you used to enjoy, or neglecting responsibilities in order to use technology.
5. Preoccupation: Constantly thinking about technology, even when you are not using it.
6. Neglecting relationships: Spending more time using technology than engaging in social activities or maintaining relationships.
7. Physical symptoms: Experiencing physical symptoms such as eye strain, headaches, or back pain due to prolonged use of technology.
8. Sleep disturbances: Having difficulty falling or staying asleep due to late-night use of technology.
9. Mood changes: Experiencing changes in mood, such as feeling anxious or depressed, as a result of your use of technology.
10. Concealing use: Hiding or lying about your use of technology, or feeling ashamed or guilty about the amount of time you spend using it.

Identifying personal triggers for technology use can be an important first step in taking control of your relationship with technology. Here are a few practical tips for identifying and managing your personal triggers:

1. Keep a log: For a few days or a week, keep track of every time you use technology, what you were doing at the time, and how you were feeling. This log can help you identify patterns in your technology use.

2. Look for patterns: Review your log and look for patterns or trends. For example, do you tend to use technology more when you are feeling bored, anxious, or stressed? This can help you identify the emotions or feelings that trigger your technology use.
3. Identify emotions: Pay attention to the emotions or feelings that tend to trigger your technology use. Are you using technology to distract yourself from negative emotions, or to enhance positive ones?
4. Notice your environment: Pay attention to your physical environment and the role it plays in your technology use. Are there certain places or situations where you tend to use technology more frequently? This can help you identify environmental triggers.
5. Take note of time: Pay attention to the time of day when you tend to use technology more often. Are there certain times of day when you are more likely to turn to technology? This can help you identify time-based triggers.
6. Be mindful: Practice mindfulness techniques, such as deep breathing or meditation, to become more aware of your thoughts and feelings in the present moment. This can help you identify triggers as they occur.
7. Identify specific apps or devices: Are there specific apps or devices that you use more frequently than others? Identifying these can help you target your technology use and manage your triggers more effectively.
8. Identify your high-risk situations: Think about the situations that make you most likely to engage in technology overuse. Is it when you're bored, lonely, or stressed? Is it when you're procrastinating or avoiding a task?

9. Ask for feedback: Talk to friends or family members about your technology use and ask for their perspective on when and how you use it. They may notice patterns that you're not aware of.

The Fear of Missing Out, or FOMO, is a powerful motivator that affects many people's use of technology. FOMO is the anxiety or apprehension that comes from the belief that others might be having rewarding experiences from which one is absent. This can drive people to stay connected to technology, often to an excessive degree, in order to stay on top of social events and other activities. In today's highly connected world, social media platforms such as Facebook, Instagram, and Twitter have given rise to FOMO. These platforms have created a constant stream of information and events that users can keep up with in real-time. However, the downside is that users can start to feel as if they are missing out on something if they are not always connected to these platforms.

One of the key reasons that FOMO has become such a significant issue in today's world is that social media platforms create an endless stream of information. Users can constantly scroll through their news feeds, checking in on their friends' activities and interests. They may also receive notifications whenever someone posts or comments on their posts, which can make it difficult to step away from the platform. FOMO can also have a significant impact on mental health. Many people who struggle with FOMO experience feelings of anxiety, loneliness, and depression. They may feel as if they are not living up to the expectations of others or that they are not experiencing life to the fullest. In some cases, this can lead to more serious mental health issues such as social anxiety and depression.

In order to identify the role of FOMO in one's own technology use, it is important to take a step back and evaluate one's own feelings and motivations. Some common signs that FOMO may be driving one's technology use include:

1. Feeling anxious or upset when one is unable to check their phone or social media accounts
2. Feeling pressure to respond immediately to notifications and messages
3. Feeling the need to constantly check one's phone, even during important events or meetings
4. Feeling envious or jealous of other people's experiences, as shared on social media
5. Feeling as if one is missing out on something if they are not constantly connected to social media
6. Experiencing negative emotions such as sadness or anger when one is unable to participate in a social event or activity
7. Finding it difficult to disconnect from technology, even when on vacation or during leisure time
8. Spending excessive amounts of time on social media or other technology platforms
9. Feeling as if one's self-worth is tied to their social media presence or the amount of likes and comments they receive
10. Neglecting real-life relationships and activities in favor of spending time on social media and other technology platforms.

By understanding these signs and symptoms of FOMO, individuals can start to take steps to address their technology use and improve their mental health. This may include setting limits on technology use, taking breaks from social media, and seeking professional help if necessary. Ultimately, it is important to recognize the role that FOMO plays in one's technology use and take steps to manage its impact on mental health. Thr fear of missing out, is a common feeling that many people experience in today's fast-paced, interconnected world. It's the sense that there is always something exciting happening somewhere, and if you're not a part of it, you're missing out on something essential. FOMO can lead to anxiety, stress, and even depression. Fortunately, there are strategies that you can use to overcome FOMO and live a more fulfilling life. Here are eight strategies to help you remove FOMO:

1. Identify your priorities: One of the most effective ways to remove FOMO is to clarify your priorities. Think about what matters most to you, and make a list of the things that bring you the most joy and fulfillment. When you know what's important to you, it's easier to let go of the things that aren't.
2. Practice gratitude: FOMO often arises from a sense of scarcity or lack, as if there's not enough to go around. Practicing gratitude can help you shift your mindset to one of abundance. Take time each day to appreciate what you have, whether it's your health, your relationships, or your job.
3. Limit your exposure to social media: Social media can be a major trigger for FOMO. It's easy to get caught up in other people's highlight reels and feel like you're missing out on something. Consider limiting your time

on social media, or taking a break altogether.

4. Focus on the present moment: FOMO is often rooted in a sense of anxiety about the future or regret about the past. By focusing on the present moment, you can free yourself from those worries and enjoy what's happening right now.
5. Embrace JOMO: JOMO, or the joy of missing out, is the opposite of FOMO. It's the idea that there's something wonderful about choosing to stay in and do something you love instead of going out and feeling obligated to do something else. Embracing JOMO can help you appreciate the value of downtime and self-care.
6. Practice mindfulness: Mindfulness is a powerful tool for managing stress and anxiety. By practicing mindfulness, you can learn to observe your thoughts and feelings without judgment, which can help you detach from FOMO.
7. Engage in activities that bring you joy: When you're doing something you love, it's hard to feel like you're missing out on something else. Make time for the activities that bring you joy, whether it's hiking, reading, or playing music.
8. Cultivate meaningful relationships: FOMO often arises from a sense of social isolation or loneliness. By cultivating meaningful relationships with others, you can feel more connected and less like you're missing out on something. Make time for the people who matter most to you, and seek out opportunities to meet new people who share your interests.

In conclusion, removing FOMO is about identifying your priorities, cultivating a sense of gratitude and abundance, focusing on the present moment, and engaging in activities that bring you joy. By practicing mindfulness, embracing JOMO, limiting your exposure to social media, and cultivating meaningful relationships, you can overcome FOMO and live a more fulfilling life.

CHAPTER FOUR

Starting Digital Detox

Setting boundaries with technology use

Technology has become an integral part of our daily lives, and it has significantly improved our lives in various ways. However, the excessive use of technology can have negative effects on our physical and mental health, social relationships, and productivity. Therefore, it is essential to set boundaries with technology use to maintain a healthy balance.

Here are some steps you can take to set boundaries for technology use:

<u>**Determine Your Goals:**</u>

The first step is to determine why you want to set boundaries for technology use. Be specific about your goals, such as improving your mental health, increasing productivity, or spending more time with loved ones. Once you have identified your goals, write them down and keep them in a visible place as a reminder of why you are making these changes. Here is a step-by-step guide to help you determine your goals during a digital detox:

Step 1: Reflect on your current life situation

The first step is to reflect on your current life situation. Take some time to think about how you are currently spending your time, what areas of your life are going well, and what areas you feel you need to improve. This reflection can help you identify the areas of your life that are most important to you and where you want to focus your energy during your digital detox.

Step 2: Think about your long-term aspirations

Once you have reflected on your current situation, think about your long-term aspirations. Where do you see yourself in five or ten years? What kind of person do you want to become? Thinking about your long-term goals can help you set more meaningful and purposeful short-term goals.

Step 3: Consider your values and priorities

Next, consider your values and priorities. What is most important to you in life? What do you value most in your relationships, work, and personal growth? Understanding your values and priorities can help you set goals that align with what you truly care about.

Step 4: Define your goals

Now it's time to define your goals. Take some time to think about what you want to achieve during your digital detox. What specific goals do you have for this period? Do you want to spend more time in nature, read more books, or connect with friends and family in person? Write down your goals, both short-term and long-term, and be as specific as possible.

Step 5: Create an action plan

Once you have defined your goals, create an action plan for achieving them. What steps do you need to take to make progress towards your goals? How will you measure your progress? Be specific and break down your goals into actionable steps.

Step 6: Set a timeline

Set a timeline for achieving your goals. When do you want to achieve each goal? Be realistic and give yourself enough time to make progress, but also set deadlines to keep yourself accountable. Consider creating a schedule or a calendar to help you stay on track.

Step 7: Review and adjust

Finally, review your progress regularly and adjust your goals and action plan as needed. Celebrate your successes and learn from your mistakes. Remember that the goals you set during your digital detox are not set in stone, and you can always adjust them based on your changing needs and priorities.

By following these seven steps, you can set meaningful and achievable goals for yourself during your digital detox and make progress towards creating the life you want to live.

Identify Your Triggers:

The next step is to identify what triggers your excessive use of technology. For example, it may be social media, video games, or work emails. Think about when and why you tend to use technology excessively and make note of those triggers. Once you have identified your triggers, come up with alternative activities that you can do instead of using technology to help you avoid overuse. Here are some steps you can take to identify your triggers:

Step 1: Keep a journal

Start by keeping a journal of your digital habits. Write down when, where, and how you use digital devices and what you are doing on them. Note any feelings or emotions you experience when you use them.

Step 2: Notice your feelings

Pay attention to your feelings and emotions throughout the day. Are you feeling stressed, anxious, bored, or lonely? These feelings can be triggers for using digital devices.

Step 3: Identify patterns

Look for patterns in your digital habits. Are there certain times of day or situations that trigger you to use digital devices more? For example, do you tend to use your phone more when you are alone or bored?

Step 4: Monitor your physical reactions

Pay attention to your physical reactions when you use digital devices. Do you feel tense, have difficulty concentrating, or experience eye strain? These physical reactions can be indicators of overuse or dependence.

Step 5: Reflect on your values

Reflect on your values and priorities. Are you using digital devices in a way that aligns with your values? Are there activities or people in your life that you are neglecting because of your digital habits?

Step 6: Seek feedback

Ask friends or family members for feedback on your digital habits. They may be able to help you identify triggers that you are not aware of.

Step 7: Experiment with changes

Experiment with changes to your digital habits to see how they affect your triggers. For example, if you tend to use your phone in bed, try charging it in another room overnight. If you tend to use social media when you are bored, try engaging in a hobby or activity that you enjoy instead.

By following these steps, you can identify your triggers and take steps to reduce your dependence on digital devices during your digital detox. Remember that identifying triggers is an ongoing process, and it's important to be kind and patient with yourself as you work towards creating healthier digital habits.

Create a Schedule:

Create a schedule that will help you manage your technology use. This schedule should include specific times of the day when you will use technology and times when you will disconnect. For example, you could schedule social media use for a specific time of day or set aside time in the evening for relaxation and meditation without technology. The key is to be intentional about when and how you use technology. Here's a step-by-step guide to creating a schedule:

Step 1: Set your priorities

Start by setting your priorities. Decide what activities or goals are most important to you during your digital detox. For example, you might prioritize spending time in nature, reading, or spending quality time with loved ones.

Step 2: Determine how much time you have

Next, determine how much time you have each day to devote to your priorities. Consider your work or school schedule, any other commitments you have, and how much time you want to spend on digital devices.

Step 3: Allocate time for each priority

Allocate time in your schedule for each of your priorities. Be realistic about how much time you need for each activity, and make sure to leave some buffer time in case things take longer than expected.

Step 4: Schedule in breaks

Make sure to schedule in breaks throughout the day. Taking breaks can help you stay focused and energized, and reduce the risk of burnout. You might schedule in short breaks between activities or longer breaks for meals or relaxation.

Step 5: Create a routine

Create a routine for your day that you can stick to. Having a routine can help you stay on track and avoid distractions. For example, you might wake up at the same time each day, have a morning routine that includes meditation or exercise, and schedule in time for your priorities throughout the day.

Step 6: Be flexible

Remember to be flexible with your schedule. Unexpected things can come up, and it's important to be able to adapt your schedule as needed. Don't be too hard on yourself if you don't stick to your schedule perfectly, and be willing to make adjustments as needed.

Step 7: Review and adjust

Finally, review your schedule regularly and make adjustments as needed. If you find that you are consistently running out of time for certain activities, consider adjusting your schedule to allow more time for those activities. Similarly, if you find that you have too much downtime or aren't being productive, consider adjusting your schedule to be more structured.

By following these steps, you can create a schedule that helps you stay focused and on track towards your goals during your digital detox. Remember that the goal is not to create a rigid or restrictive schedule, but rather to create a framework that supports your priorities and helps you make the most of your time.

Use Technology Wisely:

When you are using technology, be intentional and use it wisely. Avoid using technology for unnecessary tasks and instead focus on tasks that will help you achieve your goals. For example, use productivity apps to help you stay on task, and use social media to connect with friends and family instead of mindlessly scrolling through feeds. Using technology more wisely can be a helpful way to maintain healthy digital habits during and after a digital detox. Here are some steps you can take to use technology more wisely:

Step 1: Set boundaries

Start by setting boundaries around your technology use. Determine when and where you will use technology, and for how long. For example, you might decide to avoid technology during meals or in the hour before bedtime. Setting boundaries can help you establish healthy limits and reduce the risk of overuse.

Step 2: Prioritize meaningful activities

Prioritize meaningful activities that add value to your life. Consider using technology for activities such as staying connected with loved ones, learning new skills, or pursuing hobbies and interests. Avoid using technology simply out of boredom or habit.

Step 3: Be mindful of your intentions

Be mindful of your intentions when using technology. Ask yourself why you are using technology in a given moment, and whether it aligns with your values and priorities. Avoid using technology as a distraction or to avoid difficult emotions.

Step 4: Use technology to enhance, not replace, real-life interactions

Use technology to enhance, rather than replace, real-life interactions. For example, you might use video calls to stay connected with distant friends and family members, or use social media to share experiences and connect with like-minded individuals. However, it's important to balance your online interactions with in-person interactions and avoid becoming overly reliant on technology for social connection.

Step 5: Take breaks

Take regular breaks from technology throughout the day. This might involve stepping away from your computer, turning off notifications on your phone, or engaging in activities that don't involve technology. Taking breaks can help reduce stress and improve focus and productivity.

Step 6: Practice digital self-care

Practice digital self-care by taking steps to reduce the negative effects of technology on your physical and mental health. This might include taking frequent breaks to stretch and move your body, adjusting the brightness and blue light settings on your devices, or using apps or tools to monitor and manage your screen time.

Step 7: Review and adjust

Regularly review your technology use and adjust your habits as needed. Pay attention to how technology is impacting your life and relationships, and be willing to make changes to support your overall well-being.

By following these steps, you can use technology more wisely and establish healthy and sustainable digital habits. Remember that it's not about completely avoiding technology, but rather using it in a way that supports your goals and values.

Establish Clear Limits:

Establish clear limits on your technology use, such as setting a time limit for social media or turning off your phone during dinner. These limits will help you avoid overuse and help you maintain a healthy balance. Make sure to communicate these limits with family and friends so they can support you in your efforts to set boundaries. Establishing clear limits is an important step in managing your technology use and maintaining healthy digital habits. Here are some steps you can take to establish clear limits:

Step 1: Identify areas where you want to set limits

Start by identifying areas where you want to set limits on your technology use. This might include the amount of time you spend on social media, the number of notifications you receive, or the devices you use in certain situations.

Step 2: Determine what your limits will be

Once you have identified areas where you want to set limits, determine what your limits will be. Be specific and realistic in your limits, and make sure they align with your goals and priorities. For example, you might limit your social media use to 30 minutes per day or turn off notifications during meals.

Step 3: Communicate your limits to others

Communicate your limits to others who may be impacted by your technology use. This might include family members, friends, or coworkers. Let them know what your limits are, why they are important to you, and how they can support you in sticking to them.

Step 4: Use technology tools to enforce limits

Use technology tools to enforce your limits. This might include using screen time or app usage tracking tools, setting time limits on specific apps or devices, or turning on "Do Not Disturb" mode during specific times of the day. These tools can help you stay accountable to your limits and reduce the risk of overuse.

Step 5: Be consistent

Consistency is key when it comes to establishing clear limits. Stick to your limits as much as possible, even when it's challenging or inconvenient. Remember that setting and enforcing limits is an ongoing process, and it may take time to establish new habits.

Step 6: Review and adjust

Regularly review your limits and adjust them as needed. Pay attention to how your technology use is impacting your life and relationships, and be willing to make changes to better support your well-being.

By following these steps, you can establish clear limits on your technology use and maintain healthy digital habits. Remember that setting limits is not about completely avoiding technology, but rather using it in a way that supports your goals and values.

Involve Others:

Involve your friends and family in your efforts to set boundaries for technology use. This will help you stay accountable and make the process more enjoyable. For example, you could create a family game night or a weekly technology-free day to spend time together without distractions. Here are some steps you can take to involve others in this journey:

Step 1: Explain your goals and motivations

Start by explaining your goals and motivations for wanting to establish healthier digital habits. Let others know why this is important to you, and how it can benefit your overall well-being. This can help others understand your perspective and be more supportive of your efforts.

Step 2: Communicate your boundaries and limits

Communicate your boundaries and limits to others who may be impacted by your technology use. Let them know what your limits are, and how they can support you in sticking to them. For example, you might ask family members to avoid texting you during meals or turn off notifications during certain times of the day.

Step 3: Invite others to join you

Invite others to join you on your journey towards healthier digital habits. This might include friends, family members, or coworkers who share similar goals or struggles with technology use. Consider starting a support group or accountability partnership to help each other stay on track.

Step 4: Engage in technology-free activities together

Engage in technology-free activities together to build stronger connections and reduce reliance on technology. This might include going for a walk, playing board games, or having a meal together without devices.

Step 5: Model healthy digital habits

Model healthy digital habits for others to follow. This can include setting a positive example by using technology mindfully and in a way that aligns with your goals and values. By modeling healthy digital habits, you can inspire others to do the same.

Step 6: Seek support when needed

Seek support from others when you need it. This might include reaching out to friends or family members for accountability or seeking professional help if you are struggling to manage your technology use.

By involving others in your journey towards healthier digital habits, you can build stronger connections and create a support system to help you stay on track. Remember that everyone's relationship with technology is different, and it's important to respect each other's boundaries and limits.

Remember that setting boundaries with technology use is a process, and it may take time to establish new habits. Be patient with yourself, and don't be afraid to adjust your boundaries as needed to better align with your goals. By following these steps and staying committed to your goals, you can successfully set boundaries for technology use and enjoy the benefits of a healthier lifestyle.

CHAPTER FIVE

Strategies for reducing screen time

While technology can be helpful in many ways, it's essential to find a balance and reduce excessive screen time. Fortunately, there are many effective strategies you can use to cut back on your screen time and improve your overall health and well-being. In this guide, I'm sharing a dozen practical strategies that you can implement today to reduce your screen time, so you can feel more present, focused, and energized in your daily life :

- Set limits: Set specific times during the day when you can check your phone or computer, and stick to those limits. Setting specific times during the day when you can check your phone or computer can be an effective way to manage your screen time. To implement this strategy, start by deciding on the times during the day when you are most likely to need to use your devices, such as for work or communication with family and friends. Then, set specific time limits for each session, such as 30 minutes or an hour. To help you stick to your limits, consider using a timer or alarm to signal the start and end of each session. You can also gradually increase the amount of time between each session as you become more comfortable with managing your screen time.

- Use an app: Use an app to monitor your screen time and set usage limits. Examples include Moment, Forest, and Freedom. Using an app to monitor your screen time and set usage limits can help you become more aware of how much time you are spending on your devices. To implement this strategy, research and download a screen time monitoring app that suits your needs, such as Moment, Forest, or Freedom. These apps will typically provide you with detailed data on your screen time usage, including which apps you are using the most and how much time you spend on each app. You can then use this data to set specific usage limits for each app or session, and receive reminders or notifications when you reach your limit.

- Turn off notifications: Turn off push notifications for apps that don't require your immediate attention. Turning off push notifications for apps that don't require your immediate attention can be an effective way to reduce the number of distractions and interruptions you experience throughout the day. To implement this strategy, go into your device settings and turn off push notifications for apps that you don't need to be notified of right away. This can include social media apps, news apps, or gaming apps. By reducing the number of notifications you receive, you will be less likely to feel compelled to check your device and can focus more on the task at hand.

- Practice mindful use: Before using your phone or computer, ask yourself if you really need to use it at that moment. Before using your phone or computer, ask yourself if you really need to use it at that moment. This can help you become more aware of your screen time habits and avoid mindlessly scrolling through social media or browsing the internet. To implement this strategy, take a few deep breaths before picking up your device and ask yourself if you really need to use it right now. If the answer is no, consider finding an alternative activity to fill your time or simply enjoy the present moment.

- Keep devices out of sight: Keep your phone or computer out of sight during meals or when spending time with loved ones. Keeping your phone or computer out of sight during meals or when spending time with loved ones can help you be more present and engaged in your relationships. To implement this strategy, consider leaving your phone in another room during meals or family time, or placing it on silent mode and out of sight. By reducing the presence of your devices, you will be more likely to engage with the people around you and enjoy the moment.

- Take breaks: Take breaks from your computer or phone every 30 minutes to an hour to reduce eye strain and mental fatigue. Taking breaks from your computer or phone every 30 minutes to an hour can help reduce eye strain and mental fatigue. To implement this strategy, set a timer for 30 minutes to an hour and take a short break when it goes off. During your break, stand up, stretch, and look away from your device to give your eyes a rest. You can also take this opportunity to engage in other activities, such as taking a short walk or doing some light exercise.

- Use the 20-20-20 rule: Using the 20-20-20 rule can help reduce eye strain and fatigue caused by staring at a screen for extended periods of time. To implement this strategy, every 20 minutes, look away from your computer or phone for 20 seconds at something 20 feet away. This will give your eyes a chance to rest and refocus, reducing the risk of eye strain and headaches.

- Find alternative activities: Find alternative activities to fill the time you would typically spend on your phone or computer, such as reading a book, going for a walk, or practicing a hobby. You may also want to consider trying new activities that you have always been interested in but never had the time to explore. To implement this strategy, start by creating a list of activities that you enjoy or have always been interested in. Then, schedule time in your day or week to engage in these activities. You can also use the time you typically spend on your phone or computer to try new activities and explore your interests.

- Create tech-free zones: Create areas in your home, such as the bedroom or dining room, where technology is not allowed. Designate areas in your home where technology is not allowed. For example, the bedroom and dining room can be designated as tech-free zones. This can help you focus on activities and conversations without the distraction of technology.

- Have phone-free time: Set aside specific times during the day when you don't use your phone or computer, such as during meals or before bed. This can help you be more present in the moment and reduce the temptation to constantly check your devices. This will give you the chance to be fully present in the moment and focus on meaningful activities or relationships.

- Practice self-control: Avoid using your phone or computer when you feel bored or anxious. Instead, find healthier ways to manage these emotions. It can be challenging to resist the temptation to check your phone or computer when you feel bored or anxious, but practicing self-control is key. Instead, try to find healthier ways to manage these emotions, such as practicing mindfulness, exercising, or socializing.

- Develop healthy habits: Practice healthy habits such as exercise, meditation, and good sleep hygiene to reduce the desire to spend excessive time on your devices. Establishing healthy habits such as regular exercise, meditation, and good sleep hygiene can help reduce the desire to spend excessive time on your devices. These activities can boost your overall well-being and help you feel more energized and focused throughout the day.

Remember the benefits: Finally, it's important to remind yourself of the benefits of reducing your screen time. By disconnecting from your devices, you can enjoy more meaningful interactions with loved ones, improve your physical and mental health, and feel more present and focused in your daily life.

Alternative activities to replace technology use

Here are a few activities that you can do to replace technology use:

1. Yoga or meditation
2. Reading a book or magazine
3. Painting or drawing
4. Playing a musical instrument
5. Writing or journaling
6. Cooking or baking
7. Gardening or nature walks
8. Playing board games or card games with family and friends
9. Doing puzzles or brain teasers
10. Learning a new skill or language
11. Volunteering or community service
12. Practicing a physical activity such as sports, dancing, or yoga
13. Taking up a craft such as knitting, crochet or embroidery
14. Spending time with family and friends
15. Taking up a hobby like photography, writing, etc.

These activities can provide a sense of accomplishment and fulfillment, as well as help to improve your overall well-being. Experiment with different activities to find what you enjoy most and what works best for you.

CHAPTER SIX

Cultivating Mindfulness

In today's fast-paced world, we are constantly bombarded with information from our digital devices, which can be overwhelming and exhausting. The constant stream of notifications, emails, and social media updates can leave us feeling stressed, anxious, and disconnected from the world around us. This is where the concept of digital detox comes in - taking a break from technology to reconnect with ourselves and the present moment. One effective way to achieve this is by cultivating mindfulness, which is the practice of being fully present and engaged in the current moment. Mindfulness involves paying attention to our thoughts, feelings, and sensations without judgment, and with a curious and open mind. By focusing on the present moment and letting go of distractions, we can reduce stress, improve our mental health, and enhance our overall well-being.

Research has shown that mindfulness meditation can have a positive impact on the brain, including increased activity in areas associated with emotional regulation, attention, and decision-making. It has also been found to reduce symptoms of anxiety, depression, and chronic pain. Additionally, incorporating mindfulness into our daily lives can help us become more resilient and better able to cope with the challenges of modern life. Cultivating mindfulness and being present in the moment is an effective strategy for digital detox. By focusing on the present moment and letting go of distractions, we can reduce stress, improve our mental health, and enhance our overall well-being.

There are several practical ways to incorporate mindfulness into your daily life and practice it as a means of digital detox. Here are some ideas to get started:

- Start your day with mindfulness: Begin your day by taking a few deep breaths and setting an intention to be present in the moment. You can do this while lying in bed or sitting up straight.
- Practice mindful breathing: Throughout the day, take a few minutes to focus on your breath. Observe the sensation of the air moving in and out of your nose or your chest or belly, rising and falling.
- Take mindful breaks: Take short breaks throughout the day to pause and check in with yourself. Step away from your digital devices and take a few deep breaths, stretch, or take a short walk outside.
- Eat mindfully: When you eat, take time to savor each bite and notice the taste, texture, and smell of your food.
- Practice mindful listening: When you are in a conversation with someone, practice active listening by fully engaging in what they are saying and responding with curiosity and compassion.
- Use guided meditations: There are many free guided meditations available online or through mobile apps that can help you cultivate mindfulness and reduce stress. You can easily find one on YouTube.

Remember, mindfulness is a practice that requires consistency and patience. You may find it challenging at first, but with regular practice, it can become a natural part of your daily routine and help you achieve a more balanced and present state of mind.

CHAPTER SEVEN

Detoxing from Social Media

Identifying your personal relationship with social media

Identifying your personal relationship with social media is an important step in understanding how it impacts your mental health and well-being. Here are some steps you can take to help you identify your relationship with social media:

1. Assess your social media use: Start by taking an honest look at how much time you spend on social media each day or week. Keep track of how often you check your accounts and for how long.
2. Notice your emotions: Pay attention to how you feel before, during, and after using social media. Do you feel anxious or stressed when you are not able to access your accounts? Do you feel upset or triggered by certain types of content?
3. Reflect on your motivation: Ask yourself why you use social media. Are you looking for connection, entertainment, or validation? Do you feel pressure to keep up with others or maintain a certain image online?

4. Consider the impact on your life: Think about how social media use affects other areas of your life, such as relationships, work, and self-care. Does it interfere with your ability to focus or engage in meaningful activities? Does it leave you feeling drained or overwhelmed?
5. Set boundaries: Based on your reflection and assessment, consider setting some boundaries around your social media use. This could include limiting your time online, unfollowing accounts that trigger negative emotions, or taking regular breaks from social media altogether.

Remember that your personal relationship with social media is unique, and what works for someone else may not work for you. It's important to be honest with yourself about how social media use affects you and make changes that support your mental health and well-being.

Strategies for reducing social media use

Social media has become an integral part of our daily lives, but it can also have negative impacts on our mental health and well-being. If you find yourself spending too much time on social media and want to reduce your use, here are a dozen strategies you can try:

1. Set goals: Identify why you want to reduce your social media use and set specific goals that align with your intentions. This will help you stay motivated and focused.

2. Track your usage: Use an app or screen time feature to track how much time you spend on social media each day. This will give you a clear picture of your habits and help you identify areas for improvement.
3. Create a schedule: Set specific times during the day when you allow yourself to check social media. Stick to your schedule and avoid using social media outside of those designated times.
4. Turn off notifications: Disable notifications from social media apps to reduce the temptation to check them frequently.
5. Remove apps from your phone: If possible, delete social media apps from your phone altogether. This will make it harder to access them and reduce the likelihood of mindless scrolling
6. Take breaks: Set aside regular breaks from social media, such as a day or weekend each week. Use this time to engage in other activities that bring you joy and relaxation
7. Replace social media with other activities: Find alternative activities that you enjoy and can engage in during your free time, such as reading, exercising, or spending time with loved ones.
8. Focus on quality over quantity: Instead of trying to keep up with every post, focus on engaging with content that is meaningful to you and adds value to your life.
9. Create social media-free zones: Establish specific areas in your home or workplace where you do not use social media, such as the dinner table or during meetings.
10. Connect with people in person: Instead of relying on social media to stay connected, make plans to meet with friends and family in person.

11. Practice mindfulness: When you do use social media, practice mindfulness by being fully present and engaged with the content you are viewing. This can help you avoid mindless scrolling and reduce stress.
12. Seek support: If you find it difficult to reduce your social media use on your own, consider seeking support from a friend, family member, or mental health professional. They can provide accountability and help you stay on track with your goals.

Remember that reducing social media use is a personal journey and may take time. Be patient and kind to yourself as you navigate this process, and celebrate your progress along the way.

Tips for replacing social media use with healthier activities

If you're looking to reduce your social media use and replace it with healthier activities, here are a dozen tips to consider:

1. Read a book: Reading can be a great way to escape from the stress of social media and expand your mind. Pick up a book that interests you and make it a habit to read a little bit every day.
2. Exercise: Exercise has been shown to have numerous physical and mental health benefits. Try incorporating regular physical activity into your routine, such as going for a walk or taking a yoga class.

3. Practice mindfulness: Mindfulness is a great way to stay present and reduce stress. Try practicing mindfulness meditation, deep breathing exercises, or other mindfulness techniques to help you stay focused and calm.
4. Pursue a hobby: Whether it's painting, gardening, or playing music, having a hobby can provide a sense of purpose and enjoyment. Find something that interests you and make time for it regularly.
5. Connect with others: Social media can provide a sense of connection, but it can also be isolating. Make an effort to connect with others in person, whether it's through a hobby, a club, or volunteering.
6. Learn a new skill: Learning something new can be a great way to keep your mind engaged and improve your confidence. Consider taking a class or finding online resources to learn a new skill, such as cooking or coding.
7. Volunteer: Volunteering can provide a sense of purpose and help you connect with your community. Look for local organizations that align with your interests and volunteer your time and skills.
8. Spend time in nature: Spending time in nature has been shown to have numerous physical and mental health benefits. Try going for a hike, visiting a park, or simply spending time in your backyard.
9. Practice self-care: Self-care is important for maintaining good mental health. Make time for activities that make you feel good, such as taking a bath, practicing yoga or massage.
10. Spend time with loved ones: Spending time with loved ones can be a great way to stay connected and boost your mood. Plan a dinner with friends, have a game night with family, or simply catch up with a loved one

over the phone.

11. Travel: Traveling can be a great way to experience new things and gain a fresh perspective. Consider planning a trip to a new destination, whether it's near or far.
12. Engage in creative activities: Creative activities, such as writing, drawing, or playing music, can be a great way to express yourself and reduce stress. Find a creative outlet that resonates with you and make time for it regularly.

Remember that the key to replacing social media use with healthier activities is to find things that you genuinely enjoy and that align with your values and interests. Experiment with different activities and be open to trying new things until you find what works for you.

CHAPTER EIGHT

Detoxing from Porn

Impact of porn on our mental and sexual health

The impact of pornography on mental and sexual health is a topic of ongoing debate and research. While some individuals may view pornography as harmless, others argue that it can have negative effects on individuals and society as a whole. Here are some potential impacts of pornography on mental and sexual health:

1. Addiction: Some individuals may become addicted to pornography, which can have negative effects on their relationships, work, and mental health. Research suggests that the reward centers in the brain that are activated by addictive drugs can also be triggered by pornography, leading to a cycle of craving and use.
2. Unrealistic expectations: Pornography can give individuals unrealistic expectations about sexual experiences, leading to disappointment and dissatisfaction in real-life sexual encounters. Pornography often depicts idealized and unrealistic scenarios, which can lead to body image issues and sexual insecurities.
3. Objectification: Pornography can objectify and dehumanize individuals, particularly women, by

reducing them to sexual objects for the viewer's pleasure. This can lead to a lack of empathy and respect for others, as well as contribute to a culture of sexual violence and harassment.

4. Desensitization: Regular exposure to pornography can lead to desensitization, where individuals become less sensitive to sexual stimuli and require more extreme or novel content to achieve the same level of arousal. This can lead to a disconnect between real-life sexual experiences and the content depicted in pornography.
5. Mental health issues: Exposure to pornography can contribute to mental health issues such as depression, anxiety, and low self-esteem, particularly if an individual feels ashamed or guilty about their use.
6. Relationship issues: Regular pornography use can lead to relationship issues, including decreased intimacy, trust issues, and communication problems.

It's important to note that not all individuals who view pornography will experience negative effects, and the impact of pornography can vary depending on factors such as frequency of use, individual values and beliefs, and the content being viewed.

Identifying your personal relationship with porn

1. Identifying your personal relationship with pornography can be an important step in understanding the impact it may be having on your mental and sexual health. Here are some steps you can take to help identify

your relationship with pornography:

2. Reflect on your motivations for viewing pornography. Are you using it as a form of stress relief, to explore your sexuality, or for entertainment purposes? Understanding why you view pornography can help you gain insight into how it fits into your life.
3. Consider how often you view pornography. Do you view it occasionally, frequently, or on a regular basis? Understanding the frequency of your pornography use can help you determine whether it is becoming a problematic behavior.
4. Reflect on how pornography makes you feel. Do you feel guilty or ashamed after viewing it, or does it make you feel good? Understanding your emotional responses to pornography can help you assess whether it is having a positive or negative impact on your mental and sexual health.
5. Consider whether pornography is interfering with other aspects of your life. Are you having difficulty maintaining relationships or performing daily tasks due to your pornography use? If so, it may be having a negative impact on your overall well-being.
6. Seek support if you are struggling with pornography use. If you are having difficulty controlling your pornography use or experiencing negative impacts on your mental and sexual health, it may be helpful to seek support from a mental health professional or support group.

Remember that there is no one "right" relationship with pornography, and it is up to each individual to determine what works best for them. The key is to maintain self-awareness and make informed decisions about your pornography use based on your personal values and goals.

Strategies for reducing porn use

Pornography addiction is a common issue that many individuals struggle with. It can have a negative impact on mental and sexual health, relationships, and overall well-being. If you are struggling with pornography addiction, it is important to know that you are not alone and that there are effective strategies you can use to reduce your consumption. Here are some strategies that may be helpful:

1. Practice mindfulness: Practicing mindfulness techniques, such as meditation or deep breathing, can help reduce stress and increase awareness of your thoughts and emotions.
2. Identify triggers: Identify triggers that lead to pornography use, such as stress or boredom, and develop strategies to address those triggers.
3. Find healthy distractions: Find healthy distractions to replace the time and energy you were spending on pornography, such as exercise, hobbies, or spending time with friends and family.
4. Use website blockers: Use website blockers or content filters to limit your access to pornography websites.
5. Set boundaries: Set boundaries with your devices and internet use, such as avoiding devices in the bedroom or turning off devices during certain times of the day.
6. Change your environment: Change your environment to reduce exposure to pornography, such as removing posters or magazines with sexual content.

7. Create a plan: Create a plan for reducing your pornography use, including specific goals and strategies for overcoming challenges.
8. Practice self-compassion: Practice self-compassion and recognize that recovery from pornography addiction takes time and effort.
9. Prioritize self-care: Prioritize self-care activities, such as getting enough sleep, eating a healthy diet, and exercising regularly, to support overall well-being.

Reach out for support: Reach out to friends, family, or a therapist for support and accountability as you work towards reducing your pornography consumption.

CHAPTER NINE

Digital Detox for Children & Family

Technology has had a significant impact on family relationships in both positive and negative ways. On one hand, digital communication technologies such as texting, email, and video calls have made it easier for family members to stay in touch with each other even if they live far away. This can enhance family relationships by allowing for more frequent communication and keeping family members connected. However, on the other hand, technology can also have negative impacts on family dynamics. The addictive nature of technology, particularly smartphones and social media, can lead to disengagement from family members and a decrease in the quality of family relationships. Distractions and interruptions caused by technology can take away from family time and make it difficult for family members to engage in meaningful conversations or activities. Furthermore, conflicts may arise within families over differing attitudes towards technology use. Parents may have different rules and expectations for their children's use of devices, leading to arguments and tension within the family. Additionally, technology can lead to privacy concerns within families, such as when personal information is shared without consent or online interactions are monitored without permission.

While technology has the potential to enhance communication and bring families closer together, it is important to find a healthy balance between technology use and face-to-face interactions to maintain strong and positive family relationships. This may involve setting boundaries around technology use, creating designated technology-free time or spaces, and prioritizing in-person interactions and activities. For example, children who spend more time on devices have been found to have lower levels of empathy and social skills, which can impact their ability to form and maintain relationships with family members and others. Similarly, parents who are distracted by technology may have less patience and engagement with their children, leading to potential conflicts and strains on the parent-child relationship. Another potential negative impact of technology on family relationships is the phenomenon of "phubbing," or snubbing someone by looking at your phone instead of paying attention to them. This can cause hurt feelings and resentment within families, particularly if it becomes a pattern of behavior. Additionally, technology can exacerbate existing family conflicts or issues by providing a platform for arguments and disagreements to play out publicly or anonymously online.

On a positive note, technology can also have positive impacts on family relationships when used in moderation and with intention. For example, families can use technology to plan and coordinate activities, share photos and updates, or participate in virtual events together. Technology can also provide opportunities for learning and growth, such as online courses or educational apps. Ultimately, the impact of technology on family relationships depends on how it is used and the context in which it is used. While technology can have both positive and negative impacts, finding a healthy balance that prioritizes in-person interactions and meaningful communication can help strengthen family relationships in the long run.

Strategies for reducing screen time for children

Screen time is a significant part of many children's daily lives. From online learning and video games to social media and streaming services, screens are ever-present and can be difficult to manage. However, excessive screen time can have negative effects on children's health and development, including sleep problems, obesity, and social isolation. Therefore, it is crucial to find ways to reduce screen time and promote healthier habits. Here we will discuss a dozen strategies for reducing screen time for children :

- Establish clear rules and boundaries: Set clear rules and boundaries around screen time use, including time limits and when and where screens can be used. For example, you could establish a rule that screens can only be used for one hour per day and only after homework is finished.
- Lead by example: Be a positive role model by limiting your own screen time and demonstrating healthy behaviors. For example, you could choose to read a book or take a walk instead of scrolling through social media.

- Create alternative activities: Encourage your child to engage in alternative activities to screen time, such as playing sports, reading, or creating art. For example, you could sign your child up for a local sports team or art class.
- Encourage outdoor play: Encourage your child to spend time outdoors and engage in physical activity. For example, you could take your child to a local park or nature reserve for a hike or bike ride.
- Establish a routine: Create a daily routine that includes designated times for activities other than screens. For example, you could set aside time for exercise or reading each day.
- Use parental controls: Use parental controls to limit screen time and restrict access to certain types of content. For example, you could set up parental controls on your child's device to prevent them from accessing inappropriate websites or apps.
- Involve your child in the decision-making process: Involve your child in establishing screen time rules and limits. This can help them feel more invested in the process and more likely to follow the rules.
- Provide educational content: Encourage your child to engage in educational screen time activities, such as learning apps or educational videos. For example, you could encourage your child to watch documentaries or educational videos on YouTube.
- Monitor screen time use: Monitor your child's screen time use and adjust the rules and boundaries as needed. For example, you could keep a log of your child's screen time use to see if they are sticking to the established limits.

- Set screen-free zones: Establish areas in your home where screens are not allowed, such as the dinner table or bedrooms. For example, you could encourage your child to read a book or play a board game during family dinner instead of using screens.
- Encourage social interaction: Encourage your child to engage in social activities that do not involve screens, such as playing with friends or joining a club. For example, you could encourage your child to join a local sports team or scouting group.
- Be consistent: Be consistent with screen time rules and boundaries to establish a routine and promote healthy behaviors. For example, you could enforce the same screen time limits on weekdays and weekends to avoid confusion or frustration.

Activities for replacing technology use for children and families

Here are a few activities for replacing technology use for children and families:

1. Outdoor activities: Encourage children and families to spend time outside engaging in activities such as hiking, camping, playing sports, or simply exploring nature.
2. Board games and puzzles: Playing board games and puzzles can be a fun and engaging way for families to spend time together and exercise their minds.
3. Arts and crafts: Encouraging children and families to engage in creative activities such as painting, drawing, or crafting can be a great way to stimulate imagination and creativity.
4. Cooking and baking: Involve children in meal preparation and baking activities, which can teach

valuable life skills and encourage healthy eating habits.

5. Reading: Encouraging children and families to read books can be a great way to stimulate the imagination, develop language skills, and promote a love of learning.
6. Music and dance: Playing musical instruments, singing, and dancing can be a fun and engaging way for families to spend time together and develop creativity and physical skills.
7. Sports and fitness activities: Encouraging children and families to engage in sports and fitness activities can promote physical health and teach important skills such as teamwork and discipline.
8. Volunteering and community service: Engaging in community service and volunteering can teach children and families about the importance of giving back and instill a sense of responsibility and empathy.
9. Gardening: Planting and maintaining a garden can teach children about science, nature, and responsibility while also providing fresh produce and promoting healthy eating habits.
10. Travel and exploration: Encouraging children and families to travel and explore new places can broaden their horizons and expose them to new experiences and cultures.
11. Family game night: Setting aside a regular time for family game night can be a fun and engaging way to spend time together and build relationships.
12. Conversation and storytelling: Encouraging children and families to engage in conversation and storytelling can promote communication skills, build relationships, and promote emotional intelligence.

There are many fun and engaging activities that families can do together to replace technology use and promote healthy habits. Whether it's spending time outdoors, playing board games, or engaging in creative activities, there are plenty of ways to have fun and build strong relationships without relying on screens.

CHAPTER TEN

Maintaining a Digital Detox

Strategies for maintaining a digital detox after completing the detox

While a digital detox can be a great way to reset and recharge, it's important to maintain healthy habits and avoid falling back into old habits after completing the detox. Here we will discuss few strategies for maintaining a digital detox with practical guidance.

- Set boundaries: One of the most important strategies for maintaining a digital detox is setting boundaries. This can include specific times of the day when digital devices are not used, such as during meals or before bedtime. It can also include designating specific areas of the home as technology-free zones, such as the bedroom or dining room.
- Practice mindfulness: Mindfulness is a state of awareness that involves being present in the moment and fully engaged in the activity at hand. Practicing mindfulness can help individuals stay focused and avoid mindless scrolling on digital devices. Mindfulness techniques, such as deep breathing or meditation, can

also be helpful for reducing stress and anxiety.

- Find alternative activities: One of the best ways to maintain a digital detox is to find alternative activities to replace digital device use. This can include engaging in physical activity, such as going for a walk or practicing yoga. It can also include creative pursuits, such as painting or writing, or social activities, such as spending time with friends or family.
- Use technology mindfully: While a digital detox involves limiting or abstaining from digital device use, it's important to remember that technology can still be a valuable tool when used mindfully. This can include using apps or tools to track fitness goals or manage finances. It can also include using technology to stay connected with friends and family who live far away.
- Limit social media use: Social media can be a major source of stress and anxiety for many individuals. To maintain a digital detox, it's important to limit social media use and be mindful of how it affects mental health. This can include unfollowing accounts that cause negative feelings or taking breaks from social media altogether.
- Create a support system: It can be helpful to create a support system of friends or family members who are also interested in maintaining healthy technology habits. This can include setting goals together or checking in with each other to stay accountable.
- Be patient and persistent: Breaking old habits and creating new ones can take time and effort. It's important to be patient with yourself and persistent in maintaining healthy habits. It's also important to remember that slip-ups are normal and not to get discouraged if a digital detox is not perfect

Maintaining a digital detox can be challenging, but it's important for promoting healthy habits and reducing stress and anxiety. By setting boundaries, practicing mindfulness, finding alternative activities, using technology mindfully, limiting social media use, creating a support system, and being patient and persistent, individuals can maintain a healthy balance between technology use and other aspects of their lives.

Integrating technology in a healthy way back into daily life

Integrating technology in a healthy way back into daily life after a digital detox or period of reduced technology use can be challenging. While technology is a valuable tool, it's important to maintain healthy habits and avoid falling back into old patterns of excessive screen time. Here we will discuss a dozen strategies for integrating technology in a healthy way back into daily life with practical guidance and examples.

- Set goals: Before integrating technology back into daily life, it can be helpful to set goals for technology use. This can include specific times of the day when technology will be used, such as during work hours or for entertainment in the evening. It can also include goals for reducing screen time or increasing physical activity.
- Create a schedule: Once goals have been established, creating a schedule can help individuals stick to healthy technology habits. This can include specific times of the day when technology will be used and when it will be

put away. It can also include time for physical activity, creative pursuits, or social activities.

- Use technology intentionally: Integrating technology back into daily life involves using technology intentionally rather than mindlessly. This can include using technology for specific tasks, such as work or communication with friends and family, rather than aimless browsing.
- Take breaks: It's important to take breaks from technology throughout the day to avoid excessive screen time. This can include taking a few minutes to stretch, go for a walk, or engage in a different activity.
- Set boundaries: Setting boundaries around technology use can help individuals maintain healthy habits. This can include designating specific times and places for technology use and designating technology-free zones, such as the bedroom or dining room.
- Use technology to support healthy habits: Technology can be a valuable tool for supporting healthy habits, such as fitness and nutrition. This can include using fitness trackers or nutrition apps to track progress and set goals.
- Prioritize social connections: Integrating technology back into daily life can involve prioritizing social connections with friends and family. This can include using technology to stay connected with loved ones who live far away or using technology to make plans for social activities.
- Engage in creative pursuits: Integrating technology back into daily life can involve engaging in creative pursuits, such as writing, painting, or music. This can provide a healthy outlet for self-expression and reduce reliance on digital devices.

- Create a support system: Having a support system of friends or family members who are also interested in maintaining healthy technology habits can be helpful for staying accountable and motivated. This can include setting goals together or checking in with each other regularly.
- Practice mindfulness: Mindfulness techniques, such as deep breathing or meditation, can help individuals stay focused and avoid mindless scrolling on digital devices. Practicing mindfulness can also be helpful for reducing stress and anxiety.
- Limit social media use: Social media can be a major source of stress and anxiety for many individuals. Integrating technology back into daily life can involve limiting social media use and being mindful of how it affects mental health.
- Be patient and persistent: Integrating technology back into daily life can take time and effort. It's important to be patient with yourself and persistent in maintaining healthy habits. It's also important to remember that slip-ups are normal and not to get discouraged if a healthy technology balance is not perfect.

Integrating technology back into daily life in a healthy way involves setting goals, creating a schedule, using technology intentionally, taking breaks, setting boundaries, using technology to support healthy habits, prioritizing social connections, engaging in creative pursuits, creating a support system, practicing mindfulness, limiting social media use, and being patient and persistent. By following these strategies, individuals can maintain a healthy balance between technology use and other aspects of their lives.

CHAPTER ELEVEN

Cognitive Restructuring & CBT Self-help

One effective way to support digital detox is through cognitive restructuring techniques, which involve identifying and changing negative thought patterns related to technology use. Here we will explore some of the cognitive restructuring techniques that can be effectively useful in supporting digital detox.

Identify and Challenge Negative Thoughts:

Negative thoughts related to technology use can contribute to digital addiction and make it difficult to engage in digital detox. Examples of negative thoughts include "I can't function without my phone" or "I need to check my social media constantly." One effective cognitive restructuring technique is to identify these negative thoughts and challenge them. This involves questioning the validity of the thought, and looking for evidence that supports or contradicts it. For example, if someone has the thought "I need to check my email constantly," they might ask themselves, "Is this thought true?" or "What evidence do I have that supports or contradicts this thought?" This process can help to break down the automatic and compulsive thinking patterns that contribute to digital addiction.

Reframe Negative Thoughts:

Once negative thoughts related to technology use have been identified and challenged, the next step is to reframe them into more positive and realistic thoughts. This can involve finding alternative ways to meet the same need that technology was providing, such as seeking out social connections through in-person interactions rather than social media. Reframing negative thoughts can also involve focusing on the benefits of reducing technology use, such as more time for self-care, increased productivity, and improved mental health.

Practice Gratitude:

Practicing gratitude involves intentionally focusing on the positive aspects of one's life and expressing gratitude for them. This can help to shift the focus away from technology use and promote a more balanced perspective. One effective way to practice gratitude is to keep a gratitude journal, where one writes down three things they are grateful for each day. This technique can help to reduce stress, increase positive emotions, and promote a sense of well-being.

Set Realistic Goals:

Setting realistic goals for digital detox can help to reduce feelings of overwhelm and increase the likelihood of success. Goals should be specific, measurable, attainable, relevant, and time-bound. Examples of realistic goals for digital detox might include reducing screen time by 30 minutes per day, turning off electronic devices during meals, or taking a day off from technology each week. By setting realistic goals, individuals can take small steps towards reducing technology use, and gradually build up to more significant changes.

Develop Alternative Coping Strategies:

One reason that people turn to technology is to cope with stress or difficult emotions. Developing alternative coping strategies can help to reduce reliance on technology and promote healthier ways of dealing with stress. Examples of alternative coping strategies might include exercise, deep breathing, meditation, or engaging in a creative hobby. By developing alternative coping strategies, individuals can build resilience and increase their ability to manage stress without relying on technology.

Cognitive restructuring techniques can be effectively useful in supporting digital detox by helping individuals to identify and change negative thought patterns related to technology use. Techniques such as identifying and challenging negative thoughts, reframing negative thoughts, practicing gratitude, setting realistic goals, and developing alternative coping strategies can help to reduce digital addiction, increase productivity, and improve mental and physical health. By incorporating these techniques into a digital detox plan, individuals can regain a sense of balance in their lives and achieve a healthier relationship with technology.

Cognitive Behavioral Therapy (CBT) is an effective approach to overcome digital addiction and manage stress. CBT involves identifying negative thoughts and beliefs that contribute to unhealthy behaviors and replacing them with more positive and constructive thoughts. Here are a dozen effective CBT self-questions to help in digital detox and how to use them:

- What am I doing right now, and why am I doing it? This question helps you become more mindful of your actions and their purpose. If you are mindlessly scrolling through social media, ask yourself why you are doing it and whether there is a more productive or fulfilling activity you could be doing instead.

- How does this digital activity make me feel, and why? This question helps you become more aware of the emotional impact of your digital use. If you find that a particular app or website makes you feel anxious, stressed, or unhappy, ask yourself why and whether it's worth continuing to use it.

- What am I missing out on by using my digital device right now? This question helps you become more aware of the opportunity cost of your digital use. If you're scrolling through your phone during a family gathering or a social event, ask yourself what you're missing out on and whether it's worth sacrificing those experiences for your screen time.

- What are the long-term consequences of my digital use, and are they worth it? This question helps you become more mindful of the potential negative consequences of excessive screen time, such as reduced productivity, impaired sleep, and social isolation. If you find that your digital use is having a negative impact on your life, ask yourself whether it's worth continuing to engage in it.

- How can I create healthier boundaries around my digital use? This question helps you become more proactive in managing your screen time. If you find that your digital use is interfering with your ability to focus, sleep, or connect with others, ask yourself what boundaries you can set to reduce your screen time, such as turning off notifications, setting time limits, or designating screen-free zones.

- What values do I want to prioritize in my life, and how does my digital use align with them? This question helps you become more aware of your core values and how they relate to your digital use. If you value relationships, creativity, or self-care, ask yourself how your screen time is supporting or undermining those values.

- What are some healthy coping mechanisms I can use instead of turning to my digital devices? This question helps you develop healthier habits and coping strategies. If you find that you use your phone or computer as a distraction or a way to avoid uncomfortable emotions, ask yourself what alternative coping mechanisms you can use, such as exercise, meditation, or journaling.

- What are the underlying beliefs or assumptions that drive my digital use, and are they accurate? This question helps you become more aware of the thoughts and beliefs that contribute to your screen time. If you find that you believe you need to be connected to your devices 24/7 or that you're missing out on something important, ask yourself whether those beliefs are accurate and whether they serve you well.

- What are some positive aspects of my life that I tend to overlook when I'm focused on my digital devices? This question helps you become more aware of the positive things in your life that you may take for granted. If you find that you spend a lot of time on your phone or computer, ask yourself what positive things you're missing out on and make an effort to appreciate them more.

- What are some goals or aspirations that I have been putting off because of my digital use, and how can I work towards them? This question helps you become more goal-oriented and focused on personal growth. If you find that your screen time is preventing you from pursuing your passions or achieving your goals, ask yourself how you can make progress towards those goals despite your digital use.

- How can I hold myself accountable for managing my screen time and creating healthy habits around digital use? This question helps you become more accountable and responsible for your screen time. If you find that you struggle to stick to your goals or boundaries around digital use, ask yourself how you can hold yourself accountable, such as by tracking your screen time, sharing your goals with a friend or accountability partner, or rewarding yourself for reaching milestones.

- What are some potential triggers or obstacles that might derail my efforts to reduce my screen time, and how can I overcome them? This question helps you become more prepared and resilient in the face of challenges. If you anticipate that certain situations or emotions may tempt you to engage in excessive screen time, ask yourself how you can plan ahead to overcome those obstacles, such as by setting a plan for how you will handle those situations, or finding a support system to help you stay accountable.

How to use these questions:

To use these questions effectively, it's important to approach them with an open and non-judgmental mindset. Don't criticize yourself or feel guilty for your screen time, but rather use these questions as a tool for self-reflection and growth. You can write down your answers in a journal or discuss them with a trusted friend or therapist. The goal is to gain more awareness and insight into your digital habits, identify areas for improvement, and take action towards creating a healthier balance between screen time and other aspects of your life.

CHAPTER TWELVE

Art Therapy for Digital Detox

Art therapy is a form of therapy that utilizes various forms of creative expression as a way to promote healing and personal growth. It can be an effective tool for digital detox because it encourages individuals to disconnect from screens and engage in a non-digital, sensory experience. In this article, we will explore the benefits of art therapy for digital detox and provide practical guidance for incorporating art therapy into a digital detox routine.

Benefits of Art Therapy for Digital Detox:

- Promotes relaxation and stress reduction: Engaging in a creative activity can help to reduce stress and promote relaxation. The act of creating can be meditative and calming, providing a break from the constant stimulation of digital devices.
- Increases self-awareness and self-expression: Art therapy can help individuals to become more aware of their emotions and inner experiences. Through the process of creating, individuals may be able to express and process emotions that may be difficult to articulate verbally.

- Enhances creativity and imagination: Engaging in creative activities can help to stimulate the imagination and enhance creativity. This can have positive effects on other areas of life, such as problem-solving and innovation.
- Provides a sense of accomplishment and satisfaction: Completing a creative project can provide a sense of accomplishment and satisfaction, which can be particularly rewarding in the context of a digital detox. It can help to build confidence and self-esteem.

Practical Guidance for Art Therapy for Digital Detox :

Choose a creative activity that resonates with you: There are many different types of creative activities that can be used for art therapy, such as drawing, painting, collage, or sculpture. Choose an activity that resonates with you and that you feel comfortable with.

Create a designated space for your art therapy practice: Set up a designated space for your art therapy practice that is free from digital distractions. This could be a quiet room or corner of your home, or even an outdoor space.

Gather your materials: Gather all the materials you will need for your creative activity. This may include paper, paint, brushes, clay, or any other materials necessary for your chosen activity.

Set an intention for your practice: Before beginning your art therapy practice, set an intention for what you hope to gain from the experience. This could be a particular emotion you want to explore or a specific issue you want to work through.

Allow yourself to be present in the moment: As you begin your art therapy practice, allow yourself to be fully present in the moment. Focus on the process of creating rather than the outcome, and allow yourself to be open to whatever arises.

Reflect on your experience: After completing your art therapy practice, take some time to reflect on your experience. What emotions came up for you? Did you gain any insights or new perspectives? Reflecting on your experience can help to integrate the benefits of art therapy into your daily life.

Incorporating art therapy into a digital detox routine can be a powerful way to promote healing and personal growth. By engaging in a creative activity, individuals can disconnect from screens and reconnect with their inner selves, leading to increased self-awareness, relaxation, and creativity.

If you're new to art therapy, it can be helpful to work with a trained art therapist who can guide you through the process and help you to develop your skills. However, there are also some simple techniques that you can use to begin incorporating art therapy into your daily routine:

1. Drawing or sketching: Start by simply drawing or sketching whatever comes to mind. You don't need to have a specific plan or goal in mind - just allow your creativity to flow and see what emerges.
2. Painting: Experiment with different types of paint and brushes, and allow yourself to explore different colors and textures. You might try painting abstract designs or landscapes, or experimenting with different painting techniques.

3. Collage: Collect images from magazines, newspapers, or other sources, and create a collage that expresses your thoughts, feelings, or goals. You can also use found objects or other materials to create a three-dimensional collage.
4. Sculpture: Work with clay, paper mache, or other materials to create a sculpture or other three-dimensional object. You might try creating a figure that represents a specific emotion or experience, or simply experiment with different shapes and textures.
5. Writing and art: Combine writing and art by using words or phrases in your artwork. You might create a drawing or painting that incorporates a meaningful quote or poem, or write a story or poem inspired by your artwork.

Remember, the most important thing is to allow yourself to be creative and expressive without worrying too much about the outcome. Art therapy is about the process of creating, not just the finished product. Allow yourself to explore, experiment, and enjoy the process!

CHAPTER THIRTEEN

One-week sample detox plan

Here is a one-week digital detox plan with eight points for each day to help you reset and recharge:

Day 1 :

1. Assess your current usage: Take note of how much time you spend on your devices and what activities you engage in.
2. Set SMART goals for your digital detox: Make your goals specific, measurable, achievable, relevant, and time-bound.
3. Plan activities to replace screen time: Make a list of activities that you enjoy and schedule them into your day.
4. Create boundaries around your device usage: Identify what boundaries work best for you and stick to them.
5. Start small: Set achievable goals and gradually work towards reducing your screen time.

6. Have a technology-free meal: Avoid using devices during meal times.
7. Read a book instead of watching TV or scrolling through social media.
8. Go for a walk without your phone and focus on being present in the moment.

Day 2 :

1. Begin your day with a mindful meditation: Take a few minutes to clear your mind before checking your phone.
2. Turn off notifications on your devices to reduce distractions.
3. Take a break from social media and delete the apps from your phone.
4. Spend time with friends or family without any devices around.
5. Use a paper planner instead of a digital one.
6. Try a new hobby that doesn't involve screen time, such as painting or cooking.
7. Listen to music without any other distractions.
8. Go to bed early and avoid using devices for at least an hour before sleep.

Day 3 :

1. Plan a day outdoors and enjoy nature without any devices.
2. Take a break from email and only check it twice a day.
3. Have a conversation with someone without any devices around.
4. Practice yoga or other forms of exercise without any screens.

5. Write in a journal instead of posting on social media.
6. Listen to a podcast instead of watching TV.
7. Cook a meal from scratch without using any digital recipes.
8. Spend time in a quiet space and meditate without any distraction

Day 4 :

1. Have a screen-free morning and avoid using devices for the first hour after waking up.
2. Read a physical book instead of an e-book.
3. Take a break from online shopping and avoid using any shopping apps.
4. Spend time in nature and take a digital detox hike.
5. Cook a meal without any distractions such as TV or social media.
6. Draw or sketch without using any digital tools.
7. Listen to music and enjoy the sounds without any other distractions.
8. Play a board game or card game with friends or family instead of using devices.

Day 5:

1. Take a break from screens during lunchtime and eat mindfully.
2. Spend time in nature and go for a walk or hike.
3. Try a new physical activity that doesn't involve screens, such as dancing or hiking.
4. Practice mindful breathing exercises without any digital distractions.

5. Have a phone-free evening and spend time with loved ones.
6. Do a puzzle or brain teaser without using any digital tools.
7. Draw or paint a picture without using any digital tools.
8. Listen to a new genre of music and expand your horizons.

Day 6:

1. Take a break from social media and avoid posting for the day.
2. Spend time in nature and take a digital detox bike ride.
3. Try a new form of exercise that doesn't involve screens
4. Use a paper map instead of GPS for navigation.
5. Take a break from email and only check it once a day.
6. Have a conversation with someone in person instead of over the phone or online.
7. Cook a meal from scratch using only physical cookbooks and tools.
8. Take a break from TV and watch a movie or show without any distractions or devices.

Day 7 :

1. Have a screen-free morning and spend time with loved ones instead.
2. Take a break from social media and avoid checking it for the day.
3. Spend time in nature and take a digital detox jog or run.
4. Try a new hobby or activity that doesn't involve screens, such as gardening or hiking.

5. Take a break from email and only check it once in the morning and once in the evening.
6. Write a letter or card to someone instead of sending a digital message.
7. Listen to a new podcast or audiobook and learn something new.
8. Spend time with friends or family and have a game night or movie night without using any devices.

Mission complete.

Digital detoxes can be challenging, but they can also be rewarding. By taking a break from screens, you can reconnect with loved ones, enjoy nature, and find new hobbies and activities to enjoy. Use this one-week digital detox plan as a guide and feel free to adjust it to fit your personal needs and preferences. Remember, the goal is not to completely eliminate technology from your life but to find a healthy balance between screen time and other activities.

CHAPTER FOURTEEN

Two-week sample detox plan

Here is a two-week digital detox plan with eight points for each day to help you reset and recharge:

Day 1:

1. Unplug: Begin your digital detox by unplugging completely from all digital devices. Turn off your phone, tablet, computer, and any other devices that you use regularly.
2. Spend time outdoors: Spend some time outside in nature. Go for a walk, hike, or bike ride, or simply sit outside and enjoy the fresh air and sunshine.
3. Read a book. Choose a book that you've been wanting to read and spend some time reading it. This is a great way to relax and escape from the digital world.
4. Practice mindfulness: Practice mindfulness meditation or other techniques that help you focus on the present

moment.

5. Connect with loved ones: Spend time with friends or family members without any digital distractions. Have a conversation, play a game, or do an activity together.
6. Write in a journal: Reflect on your experiences and thoughts during your digital detox by writing in a journal.
7. Get enough sleep: Make sure to get a good night's sleep. Turn off all electronics at least an hour before bedtime to help you fall asleep faster.
8. Plan for the week ahead: Use this time to plan out your schedule for the week ahead. Make sure to include time for activities that don't involve digital devices.

Day 2:

1. Practice yoga: Start your day with a yoga practice. Yoga can help reduce stress and increase relaxation.
2. Try a new hobby: Use this time to try a new hobby or activity that you've been interested in but haven't had time for.
3. Listen to music: Listen to your favorite music without any distractions. This can be a great way to unwind and relax.
4. Cook a healthy meal: Cook a healthy meal from scratch, using fresh ingredients. This can be a great way to reconnect with the process of preparing food and enjoy the tastes and aromas of the meal.
5. Learn something new: Learn something new by taking an online course or attending a workshop.
6. Spend time in silence: Spend some time in silence, away from all distractions. This can help you feel more grounded and centered.

7. Have a device-free meal: Have a meal without any digital distractions. Enjoy your food and the company of others without the temptation to check your phone.
8. Practice gratitude: Practice gratitude by reflecting on the things in your life that you're thankful for.

Day 3:

1. Take a digital-free walk: Take a walk without any digital devices. Pay attention to your surroundings and the sensations in your body as you walk.
2. Do a puzzle: Work on a puzzle or brain teaser to help improve your cognitive skills and focus.
3. Spend time with animals: Spend some time with animals, whether it's walking a dog or volunteering at an animal shelter. Being around animals can help reduce stress and increase feelings of happiness.
4. Have a phone-free morning: Avoid checking your phone first thing in the morning. Instead, take some time to stretch, breathe, or do a quick workout to start your day off right.
5. Explore your neighborhood: Explore your neighborhood or a nearby park. Take in the sights and sounds of your surroundings without any distractions.
6. Practice self-care: Spend some time practicing self-care. This might include taking a bath, getting a massage, or doing a face mask.
7. Volunteer your time: Volunteer your time for a cause that you're passionate about. This can be a great way to connect with others and feel good about making a positive impact.
8. Spend time with family: Spend quality time with your family without any digital distractions. Play a game, do a

puzzle, or have a conversation.

Day 4:

1. Have a screen-free afternoon: Spend the afternoon without any screens. Instead, engage in activities that don't involve technology such as playing a board game, doing a craft, or going for a walk.
2. Practice deep breathing: Practice deep breathing exercises to help reduce stress and anxiety.
3. Write a letter: Write a letter to someone you care about. This can be a great way to connect with loved ones in a meaningful way.
4. Take a bath: Take a relaxing bath to help soothe sore muscles and reduce stress.
5. Practice self-reflection: Spend some time reflecting on your goals and aspirations. Write them down in a journal or create a vision board to help keep you motivated.
6. Have a tech-free night: Avoid using any technology before bedtime. Instead, read a book, meditate, or practice relaxation techniques to help you sleep better.
7. Declutter your space: Spend some time decluttering your space to create a more calming and organized environment.
8. Try a new form of exercise: Try a new form of exercise, such as swimming, rock climbing, or dancing.

Day 5:

1. Have a device-free breakfast: Avoid checking your phone during breakfast. Instead, savor your food and enjoy the company of others.

2. Spend time in nature: Spend some time in nature, whether it's hiking, camping, or simply taking a walk in the park. Being in nature can help reduce stress and improve overall well-being.
3. Have a digital-free evening: Spend the evening without any digital devices. Engage in activities that don't involve technology, such as cooking, reading, or spending time with loved ones.
4. Practice gratitude: Practice gratitude by writing down things you're thankful for. This can help improve overall well-being and increase feelings of happiness.
5. Spend time with friends: Spend time with friends without any digital distractions. Have a conversation, go for a walk, or do an activity together.
6. Create art: Engage in a creative activity, such as painting, drawing, or writing. This can help reduce stress and improve overall well-being.
7. Practice mindful eating: Practice mindful eating by paying attention to the taste, texture, and aroma of your food. This can help you savor your meals and reduce overeating. Learn a new skill: Learn a new skill, such as knitting, woodworking, or gardening.

Day 6:

1. Have a phone-free afternoon: Avoid checking your phone in the afternoon. Instead, engage in activities that don't involve technology, such as taking a walk, having a conversation, or doing a puzzle.
2. Spend time with family: Spend quality time with your family without any digital distractions. Play a game, do a craft, or have a conversation.

3. Practice yoga or meditation: Practice yoga or meditation to help reduce stress and increase relaxation.
4. Have a tech-free evening: Avoid using any technology in the evening. Instead, engage in activities that help you relax and unwind, such as reading, taking a bath, or practicing relaxation techniques.
5. Spend time in silence: Spend some time in silence, away from all distractions. This can help you feel more grounded and centered.
6. Write a gratitude letter: Write a letter expressing gratitude to someone who has had a positive impact on your life.
7. Volunteer your time: Volunteer your time for a cause that you're passionate about. This can be a great way to connect with others and feel good about making a positive impact.
8. Spend time with animals: Spend some time with animals, whether it's walking a dog or volunteering at an animal shelter. Being around animals can help reduce stress and improve overall well-being.

Day 7:

1. Have a screen-free morning: Avoid using any screens in the morning. Instead, engage in activities that help you wake up and start the day off right, such as stretching or going for a walk.
2. Connect with nature: Spend some time in nature, whether it's going for a hike, a walk in the park, or gardening. Being in nature can help reduce stress and improve overall well-being.
3. Have a phone-free afternoon: Avoid checking your phone in the afternoon. Instead, engage in activities that

don't involve technology, such as reading a book or doing a puzzle.

4. Practice gratitude: Practice gratitude by writing down things you're thankful for. This can help improve overall well-being and increase feelings of happiness.
5. Spend time with loved ones: Spend quality time with loved ones without any digital distractions. Have a conversation, go for a walk, or do an activity together.
6. Try a new hobby: Try a new hobby, such as photography, painting, or knitting. This can help reduce stress and improve overall well-being.
7. Practice mindful breathing: Practice mindful breathing exercises to help reduce stress and anxiety.
8. Go on a technology-free date: Spend quality time with your significant other without any digital distractions. Go out to dinner, see a movie, or do an activity together.

Day 8:

1. Have a device-free breakfast: Avoid checking your phone during breakfast. Instead, savor your food and enjoy the company of others.
2. Spend time in silence: Spend some time in silence, away from all distractions. This can help you feel more grounded and centered.
3. Learn a new language: Learn a new language through books, classes, or language-learning apps. This can be a great way to challenge your brain and improve cognitive function.
4. Practice yoga or meditation: Practice yoga or meditation to help reduce stress and increase relaxation.
5. Have a tech-free evening: Avoid using any technology in the evening. Instead, engage in activities that help

you relax and unwind, such as reading, taking a bath, or practicing relaxation techniques.

6. Create a vision board: Create a vision board to help visualize your goals and aspirations.
7. Spend time with friends: Spend time with friends without any digital distractions. Have a conversation, go for a walk, or do an activity together.
8. Have a screen-free evening: Spend the evening without any screens. Instead, engage in activities that don't involve technology, such as cooking, reading, or spending time with loved ones.

Day 9:

1. Have a screen-free morning routine: Engage in a morning routine that doesn't involve screens, such as journaling, stretching, or having a cup of tea.
2. Take a social media break: Avoid social media for the day. Instead, focus on being present in the moment and connecting with those around you.
3. Read a book: Spend some time reading a book, whether it's a novel, a memoir, or a self-help book.
4. Engage in physical activity: Exercise can help reduce stress and improve overall well-being. Take a yoga class, go for a run, or take a walk outside.
5. Have a device-free meal: Enjoy a meal without any technology distractions. Instead, savor your food and enjoy the company of others.
6. Spend time in nature: Spending time in nature can help improve overall well-being. Take a hike, go for a walk, or sit outside and soak up the sun.
7. Practice mindfulness: Practice mindfulness by being present in the moment and focusing on your

surroundings.

8. Do a digital declutter: Spend some time decluttering your digital life. Delete old files, unsubscribe from unwanted emails, and organize your digital devices.

Day 10:

1. Have a screen-free morning routine: Engage in a morning routine that doesn't involve screens, such as journaling, stretching, or having a cup of tea.
2. Spend time with loved ones: Spend quality time with loved ones without any digital distractions. Have a conversation, go for a walk, or do an activity together.
3. Cook a meal from scratch: Cooking can be a relaxing and satisfying activity. Try making a meal from scratch using fresh ingredients.
4. Practice gratitude: Practice gratitude by writing down things you're thankful for. This can help improve overall well-being and increase feelings of happiness.
5. Engage in a creative activity: Engage in a creative activity, such as painting, drawing, or writing. This can help reduce stress and improve overall well-being.
6. Have a tech-free evening: Avoid using any technology in the evening. Instead, engage in activities that help you relax and unwind, such as reading, taking a bath, or practicing relaxation techniques.
7. Practice mindfulness: Practice mindfulness by being present in the moment and focusing on your surroundings.
8. Have a device-free bedtime: Avoid using any technology before bedtime. Instead, engage in a relaxing activity that helps you wind down, such as reading or listening to calming music.

Day 11:

1. Have a screen-free morning routine: Engage in a morning routine that doesn't involve screens, such as journaling, stretching, or having a cup of tea.
2. Try a new hobby: Trying a new hobby can be a fun and rewarding experience. Try something you've always wanted to do, such as photography, cooking, or gardening.
3. Spend time with animals: Spend some time with animals, whether it's walking a dog or volunteering at an animal shelter. Being around animals can help reduce stress and improve overall well-being.
4. Engage in physical activity: Exercise can help reduce stress and improve overall well-being. Take a yoga class, go for a run, or take a walk outside.
5. Have a phone-free afternoon: Avoid checking your phone in the afternoon. Instead, engage in activities that don't involve technology, such as reading a book or doing a puzzle.
6. Practice gratitude: Practice gratitude by writing down things you're thankful for. This can help improve overall well-being and increase feelings of happiness.
7. Spend time in nature: Spending time in nature can help improve overall well-being.
8. Have a device-free bedtime: Avoid using any technology before bedtime. Instead, engage in a relaxing activity that helps you wind down, such as reading or listening to calming music.

Day 12:

1. Wake up without checking your phone or any other technology for at least one hour. Take this time to stretch, breathe, and mentally prepare for the day ahead. This will help you to start your day on a positive note and reduce stress and anxiety.
2. Spend 1 hour engaged in a physical activity that does not involve technology, such as jogging, swimming, or doing yoga. This will help you to get your blood flowing and release endorphins, which will improve your mood and energy levels.
3. Plan a technology-free activity that you've been meaning to do for a while, such as organizing your closet, cleaning your house, or reading a book. This will help you to achieve a sense of accomplishment and productivity without the distractions of technology.
4. Take a 1-hour break from technology during the middle of the day, and spend the time doing something that brings you joy and relaxation, such as taking a nap, meditating, or practicing a hobby. This will help you to recharge your batteries and reduce stress and fatigue.
5. Spend 30 minutes outdoors in the evening without any technology, enjoying the sunset or stars. This is a great opportunity to reflect on the day and appreciate the beauty of the natural world. You could go for a walk, sit on a bench, or do some stargazing.
6. Prepare a technology-free meal for yourself, using fresh and healthy ingredients. This will allow you to focus on the pleasure of cooking and eating without the distractions of technology. You could try a new recipe or prepare a favorite dish from scratch.
7. Spend 1 hour engaged in a creative activity that does not involve technology, such as playing an instrument, dancing, or crafting. This will allow you to express your

creativity and imagination without the limitations of technology. You may discover new talents or skills that you didn't know you had.

8. End the day with a technology-free bedtime routine, such as taking a warm bath, reading a book, or practicing mindfulness. This will help you to relax and prepare for a restful night's sleep, free from the negative effects of blue light and technology.

Day 13:

1. Spend 2 hours engaging in a creative activity that does not involve technology, such as painting, drawing, or writing. This will allow you to explore your creativity and express yourself without the distractions of technology. You may discover a new hobby or passion that you didn't know you had.
2. Turn off all technology during meals and focus on enjoying the food and company. This will help you to be present in the moment and fully appreciate the experience of sharing a meal with loved ones or friends. You'll also be able to savor the flavors and textures of the food without being distracted by notifications or screens.
3. Spend one hour outdoors without any technology, enjoying the natural environment and fresh air. This is a great opportunity to connect with nature and appreciate the beauty of the world around you. You could go for a walk, hike, or bike ride, or simply sit in a park or garden.
4. Take a 30-minute break from technology every 2 hours, using the time to stretch or take a short walk instead. This will help you to avoid the negative effects of prolonged sitting and screen time, such as eyestrain and

neck pain. It will also allow you to clear your mind and recharge your batteries.

5. Write a letter or card to a loved one instead of sending an email or text message. This will add a personal touch to your communication and show that you took the time and effort to express your thoughts and feelings in a meaningful way. It's a great way to stay connected with friends and family, even when you're not using technology.
6. Read a book or magazine for 30 minutes before bed instead of using a phone or tablet. This will help you to relax and unwind before sleep, and reduce the negative impact of blue light on your sleep patterns. You'll also be able to expand your knowledge or escape into a fictional world without being interrupted by notifications or distractions.
7. Have a face-to-face conversation with someone instead of using technology to communicate. This could be with a colleague, friend, or family member, and will help you to build stronger relationships and improve your social skills. It's a great way to practice active listening and to show that you value and respect the person you're talking to.
8. Write down 3 things you're grateful for each day in a gratitude journal. This will help you to focus on the positive aspects of your life and cultivate a sense of gratitude and contentment. It's a great way to shift your mindset and reduce stress and anxiety.

Day 14:

1. Wake up without checking your phone or any other technology for at least two hours. Take this time to

stretch, breathe, and mentally prepare for the day ahead. This will help you to start your day on a positive note and reduce stress and anxiety.

2. Spend 2 hours engaged in a physical activity that does not involve technology, such as jogging, swimming, or doing yoga. This will help you to get your blood flowing and release endorphins, which will improve your mood and energy levels. It's a great way to start your day with a burst of vitality and enthusiasm.
3. Plan a technology-free outing with friends or family, such as a hike, picnic, or museum visit. This will allow you to enjoy quality time with loved ones without the distractions of technology. It's a great way to deepen your relationships and create lasting memories.
4. Take a 2-hour break from technology during the middle of the day, and spend the time doing something that brings you joy and relaxation, such as taking a nap, meditating, or practicing a hobby. This will help you to recharge your batteries and reduce stress and fatigue.
5. Spend 1 hour outdoors in the evening without any technology, enjoying the sunset or stars. This is a great opportunity to reflect on the day and appreciate the beauty of the natural world. You could go for a walk, sit on a bench, or do some stargazing.
6. Prepare a technology-free meal for yourself, using fresh and healthy ingredients. This will allow you to focus on the pleasure of cooking and eating without the distractions of technology. You could try a new recipe or prepare a favorite dish from scratch.
7. Spend 1 hour engaged in a creative activity that does not involve technology, such as playing an instrument, dancing, or crafting. This will allow you to express your creativity and imagination without the limitations of

technology. You may discover new talents or skills that you didn't know you had.

8. End the day with a technology-free bedtime routine, such as taking a warm bath, reading a book, or practicing mindfulness. This will help you to relax and prepare for a restful night's sleep, free from the negative effects of blue light and technology. It's a great way to end the two-week digital detox program and set yourself up for a more balanced and mindful relationship with technology in the future.

Continue Practising by yourself.

CHAPTER FIFTEEN

Positive Self-affirmation

Positive self-affirmations to help with digital detox, along with ways to use them :

Positive self-affirmations are powerful tools to help shift your mindset and improve your overall well-being. When it comes to digital detox, affirmations can be especially helpful in reminding you of your goals, reducing feelings of anxiety or guilt, and reinforcing your commitment to creating healthier habits. Here are some effective positive self-affirmations for digital detox followed by some suggestions on how to use them.

"I am in control of my technology use." Remind yourself that you are the one in charge of your devices and how you use them.

"I am present in the moment." Focus on being present in the present moment, rather than getting lost in your digital distractions.

"I choose to disconnect in order to reconnect." Recognize that taking a break from technology can help you connect more meaningfully with the people and experiences around you.

"I am cultivating healthy habits." Emphasize the importance of building healthy habits that promote your overall well-being.

"I am taking care of myself." Prioritize your self-care by setting boundaries around your technology use and taking time for activities that nourish your mind, body, and spirit.

"I am creating space for creativity and inspiration." Recognize that stepping away from your devices can allow your mind to rest and recharge, leading to greater creativity and inspiration.

"I am free from the distractions of technology." Focus on the freedom that comes from disconnecting from technology and being present in the moment.

"I am creating a healthy work-life balance." Reinforce the importance of creating balance between your work and personal life, which can be disrupted by overuse of technology.

"I am prioritizing human connections." Emphasize the importance of cultivating and nurturing your relationships with the people in your life.

"I am fully engaged in the world around me." Recognize that by stepping away from technology, you can engage more fully with the world around you.

"I am in control of my time." Emphasize your ability to manage your time and use it in ways that align with your values and goals.

"I am choosing to disconnect in order to reduce stress." Recognize the impact that technology use can have on your stress levels, and emphasize your choice to disconnect in order to reduce that stress.

"I am present and focused on my priorities." Emphasize the importance of staying present and focused on the things that matter most to you.

"I am releasing my attachment to technology." Let go of any feelings of attachment or dependence on your devices, and embrace the freedom that comes from disconnecting.

"I am mindful of my technology use." Practice mindfulness around your technology use, becoming more aware of how and why you use your devices.

"I am grateful for the beauty and joy in my life." Practice gratitude for the people, experiences, and beauty in your life, recognizing that these things can be easily overlooked when you're constantly distracted by technology.

"I am in tune with my body and its needs." Tune in to your body's signals and needs, and prioritize activities that promote physical and emotional well-being.

"I am embracing the power of stillness and silence." Recognize the value of stillness and silence, and embrace these moments as opportunities to recharge and reconnect with yourself.

"I am choosing to be fully present in my relationships." Recognize the importance of being fully present in your relationships, and affirm your choice to put your devices aside and focus on the people in your life.

"I am honoring my boundaries and commitments." Emphasize the importance of honoring the commitments you've made to yourself and others, and set clear boundaries around your technology use to support those commitments.

"I am capable of making positive changes in my life." Affirm your belief in yourself and your ability to make positive changes in your life, including reducing your technology use and creating healthier habits.

To use these affirmations effectively, try incorporating them into your daily routine in one or more of the following ways:

- Repeat your chosen affirmations to yourself in the morning as part of your daily self-care routine.
- Write your affirmations down and keep them somewhere visible, such as on your bathroom mirror or next to your bed.
- Set reminders on your phone or computer to repeat your affirmations throughout the day.
- Use your affirmations as mantras during meditation or other mindfulness practices.
- Share your affirmations with a trusted friend or family member, and ask them to hold you accountable to your goals.

Remember that the power of affirmations comes not just from the words themselves, but from your belief in them and your commitment to living them out. By choosing affirmations that resonate with you and incorporating them into your daily routine, you can cultivate a more positive and intentional relationship with technology and create healthier habits that support your overall well-being.

Ending

As we come to the end of this book, I hope that you have found the information and strategies provided helpful in your journey towards a healthier relationship with technology. It can be challenging to break old habits and establish new ones, but taking the first step is crucial. By doing so, you have already taken a significant step towards improving your overall wellbeing. Taking the first step towards a digital detox may seem daunting at first, but it is important to remember the numerous benefits that come with it. By reducing the amount of time we spend on technology, we can improve our sleep patterns, reduce stress and anxiety, increase productivity, and improve our overall mental and physical health. It is an opportunity to take control of our relationship with technology and establish healthy habits that can benefit us in the long run.

However, it is important to remember that the process of digital detox is not a one-time event but an ongoing journey. It requires commitment and dedication to maintain a healthy relationship with technology in our daily lives. It may take time to establish new habits and break old ones, but with persistence, it is possible. To take the first step towards a healthier relationship with technology, it is important to start by setting clear goals and boundaries. Identify the areas of your life where technology use is most excessive, and set specific goals to reduce that use. For example, if you find yourself mindlessly scrolling through social media for hours, set a goal to limit your social media use to a specific amount of time per day.

It is also important to establish clear boundaries around technology use. For example, set specific times during the day where technology is not allowed, such as during meal times or before bedtime. By setting these boundaries, it becomes easier to maintain a healthy relationship with technology and reduce the negative effects it can have on our wellbeing. As you begin your journey towards a healthier relationship with technology, remember to be patient with yourself and celebrate small victories along the way. Even small changes can have a big impact on our wellbeing. It is also important to be aware of the potential setbacks and challenges that may arise, such as temptation to revert back to old habits or unexpected technology use in daily life. By being aware of these challenges and having a plan in place to address them, you can overcome them and continue on your journey towards a healthier relationship with technology.

If you find yourself struggling along the way, don't hesitate to seek help. As a psychologist and psychotherapist, I am available as a resource for those who need support in their digital detox journey. Whether you need help setting boundaries or managing technology setbacks, I am here to assist you in any way possible. In conclusion, taking the first step towards a healthier relationship with technology is a decision that can positively impact all areas of our lives. By implementing the strategies and recommendations provided in this book, you can reduce the negative effects of technology and improve your overall wellbeing. Remember that you are not alone in this journey, and help is available for those who need it. Let's continue to strive towards a healthier balance between technology and our wellbeing.

Contact Details of Author :

Email : contact.nitnem@gmail.com
Mobile : +91 92353 44444 (Whatsapp only)

9 798889 868552

Printed by Libri Plureos GmbH in Hamburg,
Germany